DEFINING
CONSERVATISM

DEFINING CONSERVATISM

The Principles That Will Bring Our Country Back

JONATHAN KROHN

Vanguard Press
A Member of the Perseus Books Group

Copyright © 2010 by Jonathan Krohn

Published by Vanguard Press
A Member of the Perseus Books Group

All rights reserved. No part of this publication may be reproduced, stored in a re-
trieval system, or transmitted, in any form or by any means, electronic, mechanical,
photocopying, recording, or otherwise, without the prior written permission of the
publisher. Printed in the United States of America. For information and inquiries,
address Vanguard Press, 387 Park Avenue South, 12th Floor, New York, NY 10016,
or call (800) 343-4499.

Editorial production by *Marra*thon Production Services. www.marrathon.net

Design by Jane Raese
Set in 12-point Adobe Garamond

Cataloging-in-Publication Data for this book
is available from the Library of Congress.
ISBN 978-1-59315-601-5

Vanguard Press books are available at special discounts for bulk purchases in the U.S.
by corporations, institutions, and other organizations. For more information, please
contact the Special Markets Department at the Perseus Books Group, 2300 Chestnut
Street, Suite 200, Philadelphia, PA 19103, or call (800) 810-4145, ext. 5000, or e-
mail special.markets@perseusbooks.com.

10 9 8 7 6 5 4 3 2 1

In loving memory and dedication

To Ronald Wilson Reagan, William F. Buckley Jr.,
and Barry Goldwater

*All of whom helped spark and fuel the
Conservative movement in the modern age*

Contents

BOOK THREE
Human Life

Foreword

Critics say conservatism is for stodgy and cranky old people—how about happy and enthusiastic lads? I give you Jonathan Krohn.

Jonathan is a force of nature. I first got to know him some years back, when Jonathan was ten years old and he became a regular caller to my radio show. He would call in to make a keen observation about the political issue of the day, and usually, he would tie his point to something in *The Federalist Papers* or the U.S. Constitution. Sometimes, I give extra-insightful callers a giveaway item, but was stumped as to what to give this young man. I figured I'd push the envelope a little and really challenge him and help educate him even further, so I gave him a subscription to the intellectual conservative quarterly *The Claremont Review of Books*. Jonathan did not slow down, and as he grew (and grew older), his comments became ever more incisive. He digests everything—and turns it over in his head, and then makes a whopper of a point, every time I've heard him.

Now Jonathan is fourteen. He is a full-time student, but that's not quite enough. He is also a sought-after speaker at town halls, rallies, and Tea Parties. He has been on CNN and Fox News, he's been written about in the *New York Times,* and he's been profiled in the foreign press, in newspapers from London to Budapest. When he's not speaking in public or sitting for interviews, he studies Latin and Arabic. And as if that were not enough, he captivated the annual Conservative Political

Action Conference (CPAC) last year in a three-minute speech that received more media attention than any other nonpolitician speaker I recall in 2008. Indeed, I'm always learning, too, and I began my CPAC speech last year (the day after Jonathan delivered his) in this way: "I'm Bill Bennett: I used to work for Ronald Reagan, and now I'm a colleague of Jonathan Krohn's!" It was an applause line. In a conservative audience, Jonathan is a good kid, a good man, to have on your side.

Now, Jonathan delivers to more than just a conservative audience with this book. It is a book good for both conservatives and nonconservatives. By his very being, Jonathan proves that we are a youth movement, that we are not about yesterday, and that just as Ronald Reagan would continually promise, tomorrow it is still Morning in America. With Jonathan's tome added to this year's book list, tomorrow is also a Morning in Conservatism. A fourteen-year-old writes this book that you now hold in your hands, and others think it appropriate, never mind accurate, to declare conservatism dead? Nonsense. The movement is alive, and its future strong. Here, among other things, is that proof.

There are any number of well-established stars in the conservative constellation who have defined various parts of the conservative movement and who have tried to answer the questions "What is a conservative?" and "What do conservatives believe?" Truth is, those are hard questions to answer—and no single book by a single conservative author has really tackled them specifically. Not William Buckley. Not Irving Kristol. Not George Will. Not anyone else who comes to mind. This is, in large part, because we conservatives come in different kinds, and none of us fits a single mold or can even—very often—stick to the mold we say we are in. There are libertarians, there are Straussians, there are various branches of Straussians, there are neo-conservatives, there are paleo-conservatives, there are compassionate conservatives, there are family-values conservatives, there are economic conservatives, there are social conservatives, there are even admixtures of economic liberals among the social conservatives, and social liberals among economic conservatives. The order to define this movement is tall. And yet, Jonathan Krohn, all fourteen years of him, has undertaken this tall order and done it well—weaving together, as he does, so many of the core concepts that unite so many divergent aspects and brands of this movement.

In *Defining Conservatism,* we learn a lot we did not know and we relearn a lot that we had forgotten. This is not necessarily a book diagnosing the problems in the Republican Party; rather, it is a book of politics and philosophy (in it, we get John Locke, Adam Smith, Aristotle, Thomas Jefferson, Percy Bysshe Shelley, C. S. Lewis, Ronald Reagan, and more). *Defining Conservatism* can be read quickly, but it should be read seriously. And, it should be read by every candidate for public office either wanting to call himself or herself a conservative or wanting to understand what a conservative actually believes, what the conservative basis of ideology is, and where it comes from.

Jonathan starts, helpfully, by boiling down all of conservative thought to four tenets we conservatives can all agree on (or should), regardless of our own brand, our own mold:

1. Respect the Constitution and the rule of law upon which it is based.
2. Respect life as a natural, inherent, and inalienable right for all individuals at all stages.

3. Insist on a government in its most limited format so it does not come into conflict with the individual's rights and freedoms.
4. Take personal responsibility, and work toward a system of government that makes the individual accountable for all his or her actions.

What conservative can disagree with these starting points? Of course, not all conservatives will agree with all of Jonathan's prescriptions—none of us fully agrees with any other one of us—but as baselines and analyses go, *Defining Conservatism* is smart and encourages debate.

Having known Jonathan these formative last several years, having seen him charm and challenge an audience and conduct himself as a gentleman in an interview, I consider it an honor to be asked to write this introduction. And his country should be proud as well, just as he is proud of it and serves it the way he does: as an example, as a teacher, as someone who has—at his very young age—decided to look at serious issues, take them seriously, and, at the same time, draw as much learning and life out of what his country offers as he possibly can. (His parents, too, should be honored for the young man they have raised and are raising.)

About Jonathan Krohn, it will never be said, "He had great potential." Rather, Jonathan raises the standard of potential in and for others—and makes us all the wiser for learning from him. He is a happy, cheerful, smart, and young conservative. And whatever brand of conservatism any of us is, isn't that truly the best kind?

This small but smart book is a real accomplishment, and it will raise many serious questions, the kind any country that takes politics seriously should raise. But perhaps the first question it raises is, "Okay, Jonathan, now that your book is finished, what's next?" You know it will be something. Jonathan: Go to it!

William Bennett

Preface

All too often, it seems to me, Americans get swept away by debates over policies: Should we universalize health care? Allow homosexuals to marry? Bail out homeowners with upside-down mortgages? Politicians spend a lot of time battling each other's policies, and average citizens hang all their hopes on those politicians' finding the perfect policy solution to any given problem.

While it is fine to fight bad policy ideas with good ones, it is not fine to do so without recognizing the basic underpinnings of the thought process that creates policy. I believe voters didn't understand the basic principles behind certain policies they found appealing in 2008, and that is how this country wound up with our most left-wing president: Barack Obama. Unless Americans take a step back and define their beliefs, we might have to endure another four years of his policy and its ramifications. Can America survive that?

As a conservative, I have a view of society that I believe is consistent with what our country's Founding Fathers intended, and what morality requires of us. But I am troubled by the definitions assigned to conservatism by others, who think they understand who conservatives are and what they think—but really don't. That's why I am attempting to define conservatism in a way that cannot be tweaked or manipulated from one election cycle to the next, or from one part of the country to another. I am using basic, timeless philosophical principles to define conservatism.

All policies are formed by principles. If there is no basis for one's actions, then the actions have no value, and if they have no value, then they become all but completely worthless.

It is this value and these principles that form the process of thought that is political philosophy.

This book is not about particular policies or individuals that change with every election cycle. This book is based solely and *entirely* on philosophy.

Philosophy in a vacuum is not good, for the man who makes himself philosophical yet has no true understanding of its meaning can't fathom the depth that it gives to one's decisions and opinions. Those who consider philosophy pie-in-the-sky theorizing usually dismiss it as useless.

But when philosophy is properly understood and appreciated, it is of great use to society. True understanding of pure philosophy gives one a rich understanding of key issues that affect one every day.

The conservative, as I see him, bases all of his views on society by appealing to pure philosophy. He bases his perception of the society, the individual, the marketplace and all other things on principles, logic, morality, and the rule of law. He does not base it on emotion, envy, or his own personal agenda.

I have endeavored to make this book about the credo of conservatism, the compact of conservatism, and the platform of this one movement that has changed the face of America so many times for the better.

It is not the credo of one faction, aspect, or section of conservatism, such as paleoconservatism, or neoconservatism, or libertarianism, or anything else. On the contrary, it is the credo of what I refer to as *basic conservatism.*

Basic conservatism is the uniting philosophy of conservatism. It is not the basis for *one* faction of the conservative movement, but a basis agreed on by all. In other words, in the same way that C. S. Lewis wrote about basic Christianity in *Mere Christianity*, I write on "mere conservatism."

I am committed to defining the basic ideas of conservatism that unite all true conservatives, for I believe that all factions of conservatism have no need to quarrel, because their differences are ones of policy and priority—not basic philosophy. All conservatives have the same reaction to socialist economic policies, for example. And that is what is important—perhaps never more than now, while America has its farthest left-wing president in its history!

The conservatism that I believe in is the same conservatism that President Ronald Reagan championed during the 1980s and the Founding Fathers espoused some two hundred years before that. The fact of the matter is the principles of conservatism have not changed—ever.

The conservative finds himself confronted daily by its faithful opposition, the left. The left's factions include, but are not limited to, socialism, communism, liberalism, Marxism, Stalinism, Leninism, Trotskyism, fascism, authoritarianism, martial rule, tyranny, monarchy, and, most stylish today, progressivism.

But while there are many branches of thought on the left, there is one necessary agreement among them: the desire for the continual expansion of the government's power. The conservative's truest opponent is the "government expansionist."

The conservative believes that America is naturally good; the expansionist believes that America needs more government to *make it good*. The conservative believes that the rules of the good society must be based on natural law (and the subsequent moral law); the expansionist believes that a "good" society must be based on synthetic law (and the subsequent dictated standard of men eager to meddle in other men's business). The conservative lionizes the self-sufficient individual, while the expansionist lionizes the victim. The conservative is a realist; the expansionist believes in utopianism. It is not that they do not *want* to agree, but it is that they are in constant philosophical contrast and opposition.

Many writers have defined conservatism in the past, and some of them have numbered its tenets. I, too, count a finite number of basic ideas that define conservatism:

First: Respect for the U.S. Constitution and the rule of law on which it is based.

Second: Respect for life as a *natural, inherent, and inalienable* right for all individuals at all stages.

Third: An insistence on government in its most limited format so it does not come into conflict with each individual's rights and freedoms, and remains subject to the scrutiny of the law.

Fourth: Personal responsibility, the idea that the individual is accountable for all of his actions, and *his* actions alone.

Of course, the expansionist has himself a set of principles. The first is institutionalization—the creation of a government-run society under which all individuals and private sector institutions are subjugated.

Second, the struggle of classes (and, subsequently, the Marxist change doctrine, which we will discuss close to the conclusion of this book)—a clash between different individuals so as to create the change necessary to promote the left's political agenda.

Third, victimization: encouraging the hope that the individual will find his worth in government and only by government's help.

Fourth, the synthetic law, the dictated standard, and the repudiation of natural rights—the idea that the laws of the moral compass are wrong and must be replaced by a *new,* more "efficient" standard that promotes the left's agenda.

The left's agenda is in ascendancy as I write this book in the summer of 2009, as President Obama leads the greatest offensive of government expansionism that our nation has ever witnessed.

Only conservatism can protect Americans from the loss of freedom they are certain to suffer if government expansionism succeeds. Now, more than ever, it is important to know what it means to be conservative, and what we as conservatives must do.

BOOK ONE

Basic Political Philosophy

ONE

Meditations on the Mind of a Government Expansionist

Basic Expansionism and the Modern Left's Agenda

Government expansionism is a very basic ideology. It is founded on one idea—that government might ever expand until it controls the whole society. From the oldest tyrannical dictator to the newest socialist state, the left has always promised a bigger government that is supposed to help the people.

The core of expansionist thought, this goal to create bigger government, is best referred to as *basic expansionism.* It is basic in that it is the most uncomplicated version of the ideology. Basic expansionism is, more or less, the most uncomplicated and easily understood definition of the left, of communism, socialism, fascism, progressivism, social democracy, totalitarianism, and syndicalism, among others.

Basic expansionism is not the exclusive agenda of any particular brand of leftists—moderate, extreme, or somewhere in between. This expansionist thought is the drive of *all* leftists, in *all* senses, and in *all* cases. If one is a basic expansionist, then one is merely a *leftist* in the most general sense. The degree and kind of leftism is completely determined on the basis of how a person takes the initial charge of expanding government.

Every generation spans a new view on basic expansionism that emerges as its dominant face, and the current day is no exception.

Today we find that many left-wing individuals call themselves "progressives" but are actually rooted in the retro teachings of Marxism. Of course, since Karl Marx first penned his famous *Communist Manifesto* with Friedrich Engels, its ideas have morphed into a number of versions and inversions.

Take, for example, the unionization or syndicalist principles of Leon Trotsky, as opposed to the militant principles of Joseph Stalin. Syndicalism is an idea perfected by communism, which states that after the economy is turned into part of the state, it can then be redistributed to the workers—and, more specifically, to the labor unions. Trotsky believed that by mobilizing the labor force of a nation, the Marxist "revolution" would happen more quickly and become more effective. Moreover, he believed in redistributing not only economic power to the unions, but also political power.

Stalin—who was disowned by many expansionists, including Trotsky—crafted a most pointed angle on an already extreme view. He used his power to put his opponents in prison camps, to kill off hundreds of millions of people for no justifiable reason, and generally to get his way in whatever he wanted. The totalitarian thinker—think Stalin, Fidel Castro, and Kim Jong Il, etc.—has no problem with oppression and aggression; in fact, such a thinker considers it necessary.

Since there are so many versions of the Marxist state, discussion is best limited to Marxist expansionism, on which all modern expansionists can generally agree.

Marxian Law and the Synthetic Law on Which It Is Based

There are five sectors within the society that any ideology must fully address:

1. *Morals:* the code that one uses to discern right from wrong, the application of which is considered one's "ethics"
2. *Natural law:* the basis of logic and morality
3. *Written law:* law codified by a society and capable of being judged by a court; hopefully, the moral law is here applied, since the national citizenry is forced to obey it by government
4. *Social theory:* the aspects of society that directly affect the daily life of the individual
5. *Economics:* the financial aspects of both the state's government and the individual's fiscal affairs

The written law is also considered to be the rule of law that a nation observes. The modern left believes that this rule by law is fallacious and, thereby, must be succinctly denied. Why?

This is because the idea of a rule of law gets in the way of governmental expansion. As it is, the rule of law is itself applicable to both the people and the government in the same manner. Law is blind. It cannot, should not, and truly *must not* differentiate between government and the people. If it were to differentiate between the two, then law as a basic principle that applies to all would be rendered meaningless. A government that oversteps its legal boundaries should be restrained and penalized. How can expansionists ever inflate government to its fullest extent if government adheres to the rule of law? They cannot!

Furthermore, the idea of a moral view is also seen as an absurdity by expansionists. The moral view states that there is both a "good" and a "bad" and that this is a standard which each individual and each society must acknowledge. Hence, in addressing morality, the expansionist runs into the same problem encountered with the rule of law: A *true* moral standard could not be replaced by an all-controlling government. Hence, the expansionist must deny there is a true moral standard that is knowable. In denying both the whole rule of law and the moral law, the expansionist has, in turn, denied the all-encompassing natural law. This means that the expansionist believes that there is not only no single standard of morality or legality, but also no *natural* standard of reality whatsoever. Hence, because there are now no standards, the expansionist is unchecked in a society free from laws that would otherwise protect it.

This anarchy is desirable for a government expansionist. In a Marxist totalitarian state, for example, in which the society is completely controlled by the government, the state's law itself becomes government. Hence, a law is always present, and if the Marxist wants to turn this anarchy to an advantage, he or she must concoct a *new* law to replace the natural law that was usurped.

The law that is used to replace the rule of law and morality is what I refer to simply as the *synthetic law.*

What is this synthetic law based on, exactly? There are a few rules that make up the essence of the synthetic law:

1. Anything that is a part of the synthetic law must be "man-made." Synthetic laws are therefore limited only by human

imagination instead of naturally occurring rationality and morality. Of course, the synthetic legislator is always congenial to expansionist philosophy, since the two are tied.

2. If expansionists are not to be tied down in adherence to a law or principle, they must not be tied down to *their own* law and principle! Hence the law must always be flexible to suit expansionist needs. Synthetic law is therefore relative—not fixed, as the natural law is.

3. Synthetic law's relativism is used to further the expansionist agenda. Hence, something that benefits the continued expansion of government, but is considered illegal by the synthetic law, must be become legal within that case. Anything that hinders or opposes expansionism must be illegal to the fullest extent of synthetic law.

4. The synthetic law can be continually written, rewritten, and revised. Unlike the natural law and the subsequent moral law, which never change, the synthetic law must always change when it is beneficial to the expansion of government. Hence, law to the expansionist is always living. (You will often hear expansionists describe the U.S. Constitution as a "living, breathing document"; this is but another phrase for "relative.")

Why is synthetic law so important to understand? Because Marxian law relies on synthetic law to arrive at the following dangerous conclusions:

1. All laws must be beneficial to Marxist revolution.
2. All laws must be beneficial to the creation of more power for the state.

The left's interpretation of the law is also referred to as *legal positivism:* the idea that government and its interest is the *ultimate law.*

Revolutionism

Karl Marx and Friedrich Engels wrote in the *Communist Manifesto:* "Freeman and slave, patrician and plebeian, lord and serf, guild-master and journeyman, in a word, oppressor and oppressed, stood in constant opposition to one another, carried on an uninterrupted, now hidden, now open fight."[1]

This "opposition," this contention, this "fight," this "class struggle"—as Marx and Engels at one point call it—is the justification for all expansionism. There is a battle, proclaims the Marxist, raging between the rich, successful, and independent capitalist, or the "bourgeoisie," and the so-called poor, or the "proletarian," that is the cornerstone of society.

This battle, the Marxist explains, must come to a fruitful end: It must produce a new state, a new class, and a new society. Furthermore, this new society must adhere to expansionist principles and must be governed by expansionist laws. Revolution, for the Marxist, is the means to expansionist ends.

But in order for any struggle, revolution, or fight to occur, there must be opposition. The expansionist must find an enemy. This enemy must be the antithesis of everything that is government expansionism; instead of following a synthetic law, the opponents must adhere to *natural law.* Instead of Marxian law, they must believe in *traditional rule of law;* instead of institutionalization, *individualism;* and instead of state economic collectivism, *economic freedom and a free market in general.*

The Marxist finds opposition in the successful capitalist individual, who more than likely embodies this respect for natural law and independence from government.

In order to battle the successful capitalists—whom the Marxist often refers to as the *bourgeoisie*—the expansionist must find a class to pit in opposition. The Marxist preys upon the working class within the so-called proletariat. Whether it is true or not, the expansionist argues that the bourgeoisie have oppressed the proletariat; thus, the bourgeoisie must be obliterated.

Marxists claim that the successful capitalist is truly an evil to society because the capitalist gets *more* money than other individuals and hence must be destroyed. In this manner, the expansionism tries its hardest to make the working class the *expansionist* class, identifying itself as the worker's advocate.

Marx and Engels lay their cards on the table: "In depicting the most general phases of the development of the proletariat, we traced the more or less veiled civil war, raging within existing society, up to the point where that war breaks out into open revolution, and where the violent overthrow of the bourgeoisie lays the foundation for the sway of the proletariat."[2]

Expansionists believe that not only is revolution necessary, but it is also inevitable. They believe, or at least claim to believe, that the working class and the successful capitalists are bound to collide in an ugly mess that will lead to the Marxian revolution of expansionist dreams.

But this "violent overthrow of the bourgeoisie" means the violent overthrow of freedom. Since the successful capitalist is the complete opposite of everything the Marxist admires, then it only follows that vanquishing capitalism defeats everything that is not consistent with Marxist thought. Freedom, independence, liberty, the rule of law, and individualism are all destroyed, both in fact and in the mind of the expansionist, when successful capitalists are themselves destroyed.

The Marxist's Ideal Citizenry

The key to the ideal Marxist-expansionist citizenry is *manipulation*. To politically manipulate is to weave into the minds of unwitting individuals a thought pattern created for the achievement of some political goal. In this manner, the politically manipulated citizen becomes an aid—a mere foot soldier in one's ideological war.

The expansionist's ideal citizen must be capable of being molded however the expansionist wants. If not so gullible, then the citizen could deviate from pure expansionist philosophy. Thus the person's mind must not only be dominated by leftist thoughts and hate for the left's enemies, but also be malleable enough for the left to change its direction whenever desirable.

The faith of this ideal citizen must be rooted in the state's leadership. If the people place their faith in freedom, liberty, human rights, or some other anti-expansionist ideal, then they become prone to deviate from expansionist thought. In this manner, government—which must be expanded in order for expansionism to achieve its fullest fruition—must truly become itself an object of praise, devotion, and the people's hopes and dreams. The more the individual devotes himself or herself to the goodness of government, the more the government is able to gain power.

In this manner, the ideal citizen of expansionism is one whose mind is completely, passionately, and dynamically consumed by the expansionist agenda and whose faith is put completely in the system of government. Thus we can rightfully say that the expansionist's ideal citizens find their complete worth within government.

Who fulfills all these criteria best? This individual is the *victim*.

Victims base their view of society on the idea that government is all that they need. They believe that they are *entitled* to live a comfortable life without any inconveniences getting in the way. In this manner, they believe that when they are faced with an inconvenience, it is the government's job to fix it. The victim feels that the role of government is to ensure that the individual is not insulted and that no indecency is done by him. The victim ensures that government expansionists will always feel needed. Of course, by the term *victim,* I'm not referring to victims in the typical incriminating sense of the word—the individual whose life and rights have been *truly* violated, such as a car crash victim, a robbery victim, and so forth. On the contrary, I'm referring to individuals who consider themselves victims in the sense that they believe government has not done *enough* for them.

The idea of being a victim is not as much a state of an individual's life but more of a viewpoint, a thought pattern, or an ideological standpoint. No individual is born a victim, but it is a state of mind and a way of thinking encouraged by the left's unquenchable desire to make all society feel a *need* for governmental interference within the individual's life. For this reason, I prefer to reference the idea of the victim as the *victim mentality.*

Furthermore, the victim specifies himself or herself as some-one whose ideological stances can be summed up in the phrase that the cure for the problems within our society is the involve-ment of more government *in the society.*

Maybe the most evident supporter of this mentality within our society is the American Civil Liberties Union (ACLU). The ACLU has participated in numerous cases throughout the United States that have greatly induced individuals to embrace the thought pattern of victimization—from cases on the "ille-gality" of school prayer, to cases on the "illegality" of excluding certain individuals from your organization. Moreover, the ACLU has as part of its mission statement the stated goal of protecting the unfortunate members of society, naming the fol-lowing plan as part of *this* great mission: "The ACLU ... works to extend rights to segments of our population that have tradi-tionally been denied their rights, including ... prisoners."[3] The poor, pitiful prisoner who has wronged another is now a *victim* himself! This is the victim mentality at work in the minds of trial lawyers: To the legal busybodies at the American Civil Lib-erties Union, there is an inexcusable wrong being done on the part of American legality that violates the rights of prisoners.

Utopianism

One of the most perverted aspects of government expansionism is its optimism that everything will improve the more govern-ment is expanded. The leftist hopes dearly that the revolution will be effective and not just sheer political jargon. This nervous hope stems from the fact that the revolution is based on some-thing that is nonfactual and irrational: expansionist thought.

There is no law, no structured system, not even a moral *stan-dard* that can truly be classified as the basis of revolutionism, because the expansionist denies *all* set standards. All the philo-sophical hopes and dreams of the expansionist are a hypothesis that cannot truly be tested against reality.

So expansionism must create a substitute for *all* reality. If it denies the natural law, the moral law, the rule of law in general, and so on, it has utterly denied all reality. Expansionism's reality becomes subjective—the way things *should be,* according to each individual—instead of objective, the way things *are.*

In this manner, the expansionist becomes an adherent to a philosophical feature known as *utopianism.* Utopianism is itself an unattainable political, social, or fiscal system that is a paradise on earth—too good to be true. Expansionists believe that gov-ernment can be big while people live good, natural lives. Of course, the abolishment of natural rights and freedoms, the moral law, the natural law, and the rule of law in general makes it impossible for such a "natural" life to be lived.

All utopias lead to dystopias, in fact, in which everything is desolate and horrible.

Since utopias are synthetic and not natural, they can only lead to conclusions that are not based within the natural laws. What might have been moral will become immoral. And what might have been helpful will become harmful.

Recall George Orwell's picture of society in *1984,* in which the national party's motto read, "WAR IS PEACE. FREEDOM IS SLAVERY. IGNORANCE IS STRENGTH." It was a society in which the natural definitions of words as basic as *freedom* and *strength* were twisted. That was utopia for the government of *1984.* The expansionist government, no matter how overbearing it is on the people, will always see the inevitable dystopia as a utopian society.

The goals of the retro-Marxist/government expansionist utopia are clearly outlined: Seeing as the successful capitalist is the opposition and that a working class is supposedly "helped" by the expansionist, we find that—first—the left embraces what one might refer to as state economic collectivism, the idea that all wealth must be put into one big pot and redistributed via the government's prying hand. This theory was referred to by Karl Marx: "From each according to his ability, to each according to his needs!"[4] Moreover, the left embraces this idea because—if government is in itself positive in legal theory—all society gets its wealth and freedom simply by grant of government. Thus, the money of each individual is already the government's *to begin with*—by philosophical application.

Furthermore, the left embraces what one might refer to as judicial and legislative interventionism and institutionalization; this is the theory that stems from legal positivism, which states that—if government is *the ultimate law*—then *it* must *fix* society and its woes.

TWO

Conservative Philosophy
in General

The Basis of Conservative Philosophy

Why do we as conservatives believe what we believe?

Is it because we are hopelessly nostalgic in our ideological perspectives? Is it because we hold on to the past with a hand that will not let go? Do we try to force our moral views on all other individuals? How do we conclude that conservative values lead us to any better conclusion than government expansionism?

As Plato once wrote in his masterpiece *Laws,* "because you have gone back to first principles you have thrown a light upon the argument."[1] Plato here reflected on a fact of life: Principles reflect one's personal perception.

We often take an extra step and ask another question: How does an individual come to an ideological perspective? The question is a valid, sound, and important one. Plato himself acknowledges the validity of the question when his "Athenian Stranger" character asks for not merely legislative stances, but also the origins of laws themselves.[2] In other words, to fully understand someone's conclusion, one must understand the steps leading to the conclusion.

Three basic sectors lead to the conservative perspective: logic, morality, and history. Moreover, these principles are unique to conservatism. Government expansionists are afraid of these three things; they shirk from them, because, after all, if they are confined to logic, then their ideology is confined as well. If they are confined to morality, then they are ideologically confined to adhere to a moral compass.

But if the government is to expand to the fullest extent, worries the government expansionist, there must be no boundaries. Boundaries only penalize a government as it tries to expand. Moreover, de facto boundaries—such as defining what is moral and what is logical—affect more than just one sector of society as a normal piece of legislation does. They can change one's entire perception of life.

Conservatism's uniqueness in these three areas works to its advantage. Logic, morality, and history open doors to a successful society that the government expansionist's ideals of anti-individualism and progovernmental institutionalism through class warfare cannot bring to the table. The free market, for example, is a solution employed by conservatism because of capitalism's logical, moral, and historical successes, yet it is downplayed by the government expansionist because the free market *promotes* individualism, *diminishes* the governmental institutionalization of society, and does not aid, whatsoever, in "the struggle of classes."

Logic, morality, and history are key to conservatism; what's more, the understanding of each of these individual philosophical ideals might be even more influential to the conservative perspective. The conservative ideological identity is entirely upheld by these three great societal pillars. Their influence on conservatism is not only relevant but also important for every conservative to learn and comprehend.

The Natural Law and Logic

Why is logic so critically important to conservatism? Logic is important to conservatism because it, by nature of its principle, creates a rational basis of facts for the conservative ideology.

Often, conservatism is maligned as the ideology of the "old white male," and in saying such, its opponents demonize conservatism as being out of touch with the average citizen.[3] But the fact is, conservatism is more in touch than any of its opponents.

This idea of a reality of conservatism (seen through logic) is more aptly described as *realism*. Realism is defined by the *Stanford Encyclopedia of Philosophy* as being based on two things, "existence ... [and] independence. ..."[4] Conservative realism (when seen through logic) creates a state of mind in which one sees society through the idea that the state of an object's existence is factual and true, and that what exists is not changed because of the thought of any individual human being.[5]

This goes to the heart and soul of the conservative-versus-government expansionist battle.

Because conservatives are realists, they believe that the laws of nature say all human beings are independent of one another and that there are facts that support this. The left says, however, because of its basic ideological attachment to utopian philosophy, that all things *must* work together to achieve *the government's goal of total control*.

The difference is in the individual.

Government expansionism holds that everything pivots on the government, while conservatism holds that everything pivots on the natural law of independence by which all human beings are naturally free and, similarly, *want* to be free.

The government expansionist replaces *natural law* with *synthetic law,* thereby denying logic its rightful place as the supreme ruler of the mind and upholding government in its place.

What is this natural law?

Natural law is the basis of logic. It is the principle that all facts are rooted within nature; for example, the fact that an apple falls *downward* from a tree is rooted within the principle of nature that is gravity. Thus, it is the application of fact to thought.

The principle idea of natural law as it relates to human civilization is that all society is based on a standard, all law is based on a standard, and all thought in general is based on a standard of reasoning and rationale. This standard is in itself the natural law.

John Locke discussed this idea in his "Essay Concerning Human Understanding" as "something that we, being ignorant of, may attain to the knowledge of, by the use and due application of our natural faculties." Locke, being the empiricist that he was, is primarily pointing to the idea that the natural law is the basis of society that we can learn via experience.

Hence, realism is itself a manifestation of the natural law, a view that all things that are true by nature are certainly true within reality. Thus, we can better state that the natural law is more than simply the basis of logic. It is also *reality.* And we can also state that reality is the basis of logic.

Moreover, this law of nature is itself much deeper. Locke writes in his *Second Treatise on Government:* "The *state of nature* has a law of nature to govern it, which obliges every one: and reason, which is that law [i.e., the natural law] teaches all mankind, who will but consult it, that being all *equal and independent,* no one ought to harm another in his life, health, liberty, or possessions." This is the thesis of logic and of conservatism.

But if the natural law—as I have mentioned and as John Locke has stated—is in itself the manifestation of reality, then reality itself becomes more than a view of what one sees. Reality is the truths held within the natural law. Hence what is real is only what is true within society. This—what Locke referred to as the "state of nature"—is a key truth of society and the natural law; in this manner, we find an affirmation of the natural law's relation to this important aspect of reality.

Of course, the natural law and its properties are equally as practical as they are philosophically important.

If conservatism is truly the realist ideology, then it must be the more factual ideology. Moreover, if government expansionism is truly the utopian ideology, then it must, in turn, find itself the *less* factual ideology. What's more, realism creates a logical argument for conservatism that is unbeatable: Conservatism believes in realism, realism is factual; therefore, conservatism believes in facts. While utopianism creates an argument for government expansionism, utopianism is generalized and hypothetical, and therefore, government expansionism believes in things that are generalized and hypothetical.

Conservatives are realists; make no mistake about that. This is not to say in the least that conservatives do not, at least in part, believe in ideals or believe in idealistic tenants. Quite the contrary! Logic warns against being too idealistic. Conservatives balance their ideals with reality and fact. If conservatives were to be *wholly* idealists, then they would demolish the whole truth factor of conservatism. But if they are realistic in their ideals, conservatism's claims remain valid and their principles remain solid. In other words, conservatism is an ideology that holds to ideals, but such ideals must always be balanced by logic and reality.

Morality

Often we refer to things within reality—things within the natural law—as good things. We say that one thing is good and another thing is bad. We refer to one outcome as better and another as worse. It is evident, however, that *good* only makes sense inasmuch as it relates to *bad,* and that *better* only has meaning inasmuch as it relates to *worse.* By what standard are all of these relative terms understood?

The basis of this answer is something often referred to as *morality.* But what do we consider moral, and how is it so? More often than not, we consider morality relative to our perception and opinion. We consider one person's internal moral compass part of one sector of society's perception, and another's moral compass part of another sector of society's perception. But to say such means that my version of good and bad could very well be different from yours.

The conservative bases an understanding of morality not on opinion, but on reality, and thus on the natural law. And, in this manner, morality must be a naturally known fact of society.

C. S. Lewis wrote on this:

This law was called the law of nature because people thought that every one knew it by nature and did not need to be taught it. They did not mean, of course, that you might not find an odd individual here and there who did not know it, just as you find a few people who are colour-blind or have no ear for a tune. But taking the race as a whole, they thought that the human idea of decent behaviour was obvious to every one. And I believe they were right. If they were not, then all the things we said about the war [World War II] were nonsense. What was the sense in saying the enemy were in the wrong unless Right is a real thing which the Nazis at the bottom knew as well as we did and ought to have practiced?[6]

Lewis's statement here is not that we are born *moral,* but that each individual learns through reason a *sense* of what moral is. For example, we know from an early age that lying is bad. But if there is no moral compass, and if each human being does not have a moral compass—or even if the individual's perception of morality is based on opinion—then all accusations about lying come to nothing. Lying could be perfectly acceptable to some and not acceptable to others. Lying becomes acceptable, and the orthodox liar (if there is such a thing) becomes equally as welcomed as the orthodox truth-teller.

What's more, there is no justice in such a society. If there is no moral compass, then we are free to do anything. Moreover, if there is no moral compass, then a rule of law is pointless because there is no *absolute* right and wrong, as dictated by ideals such as "Thou shall not steal" or "Thou shall not murder."

In other words, a society in which there is no moral compass leaves us with this: No law. No justice. No beliefs. Of course, such a look at a society that has no moral compass looks quite unappealing to most.

C. S. Lewis wrote: "Whenever you find a man who says he does not believe in a real Right and Wrong you will find the same man going back on this [in] a moment. He may break his promise to you, but if you try breaking one on him he will be complaining 'It's not fair.'"[7]

Of course, many people beg for answers as to the necessity of acknowledging the moral compass. The answer is simple: If there is a moral right and wrong, then it is key that we strive to do what is right. If there is a unique, definite, and strong moral rule, then it is only relevant that we know, use, and promote it. Therefore, conservatives believe that it is only moral to have a rule of law. It is only moral, according to the realist conservative, that there be boundaries for government and freedoms for people, as well as laws that reflect what is truly moral and what is truly good. This idea that morality is made up of set standards is known in and of itself as *the theory of categorical morality.*

Some in the governmental expansionist camp use—in a very untruthful manner—such a belief in a rule of law as an excuse. If it's a law, these people ask, then by morality's relationship to the rule of law, isn't it automatically good? This question is twisted. The rule of law, just like all other aspects of society, is as open to scrutiny as any other aspect of human society. Just because a government official passes a law does not make it justifiable. This is why government expansionism cannot have a moral compass as a centerpiece of its ideology. The moral compass limits the goodness of government to what is *truly* right, as well as making the government open to scrutiny, and according to utopianism and the other aspects of the government expansionist ideology, government *must* be good all the time. Moreover, the preaching of morality and religion is seen by the government expansionist as part of the evil advancement of the bourgeois perspective.[8] This puts morality in the crosshairs of the government expansionist as something expansionism needs to destroy just as much as its proposed promulgator.

BOOK TWO

The Rule of Law and
the American Constitution

THREE

Defining Rule by Law

Since happiness is an activity of the soul in accordance with perfect virtue, we must consider the nature of virtue; for perhaps we shall thus see better the nature of happiness. The true student of politics, too, is thought to have studied virtue above all things; for he wishes to make his fellow citizens good and obedient to the laws.

—Aristotle, *Nicomachean Ethics,* Book I

What Is a Rule of Law?

To put Aristotle's observation into other words, a rule of just laws is good, and obedience to such laws is ethical and virtuous and leads to happiness.

Conservatives believe that a rule of law is key to a good society. If society is meant to prosper, if society is meant to succeed, if society is meant to be just, if society is meant to be moral, and if society is meant to remain stable, then there must be a set system of laws that dictates the good and the bad and that gives the law both impartiality and Aristotle's "perfect virtue."[1]

To the conservative, law must be, as Aristotle implied, an institution of morality and logicality. To the government expansionist, on the other hand, law must promote the expansion of government into society, the destruction of the individual, and "the struggle of [the] classes."[2]

One of these two perspectives on law thrives on the institution of government; the other thrives on the natural law.

Why is the natural law so integral to the rule of law? Because natural law is the basis of a rational look at the facts of society, it only follows that the denial of the natural law denies the rationality of the law; when you deny logic and morality a place in the law, you create a rule of law pivoting not on the difference between right and wrong, not on anything reasonable, *not on* realism, not on facts, but on personal opinions.[3]

Reality and morality must be the two underpinnings for the rule of law. This is simply because if there is no reality in the law, then the law is pointlessly illegitimate, unreasonable, and nonfactual. If there are no realistic perspectives within the law, then it becomes a simple figment of human imagination and not a by-product of the laws of nature.

If there is no morality, likewise, the law is shallow. After all, the lack of morality leaves one without a basis for what is right and what is wrong. Such baselessness turns the law, once more, into a piece of *opinion* instead of a branch of facts. No stated right or wrong turns criminals into unfortunate people who are not really *wrong* in what they did but merely *thought to be wrong*. No right in society means that justice has no goodness over injustice and anarchy.

In a judicial system that is often metaphorically referenced as "blind," such a view of justice changes without morality; after all, how can justice be blind when right and wrong are merely figments of the imagination, and a judge's decision is not based on any set facts of good and bad but on his or her personal opinion at the time? The fact is, such a society cannot pride itself on a systematic love for judicial impartiality.

Black's Law Dictionary describes justice as "the constant and perpetual disposition to render every man his due."[4] *Black's* continues: "In the most extensive sense of the word 'justice' differs little from 'virtue,' for it includes within itself the whole circle of virtues."

In order to make a proper distinction between the two, *Black's* draws a conclusion: "Yet the common distinction between them is that which, considered positively and in itself, called 'virtue,' when considered relatively and with respect to others has the name of 'justice.' But 'justice,' being in itself a part of 'virtue,' is confined to things simply good or evil, and consists in a man's taking such a proportion of them as he ought." Justice and the rule of law must not be divorced from the moral compass, realist thought, and all other aspects of the natural law. It is the difference between good and evil that defines justice.[5]

In this manner, the differentiating factor between the conservative view of justice and government expansionist pure positivism is the moral compass, virtue, and the natural law.

Of course, many in the government expansionist camp claim that the conservative's view on justice does not sympathize with the average citizen well enough. There needs to be more *empathy* in judicial philosophy, they exclaim.

Of course, this is neither factual nor logical. If we are to be empathetic in our statements on the law, then we are not being just at all, but *thoughtful*. We are to *feel for the citizen*. Instead of thinking in terms of what is right and what is wrong at all stages, we are destroying the entire basis for justice and the system itself.

Aristotle crystallized it: "The law looks only at the distinctive character of the injury, and treats the parties as equal."[6] In other words, it is the goal of the law to look at the moral nature of the issue set before it, not at the individual or individuals whose actions are in question. Conservatives believe that justice is justice, and it must not be confused for our emotional attachments. For this very reason, impartiality is a necessary trait of justice.

The difference between virtue and justice lies in this: Justice is the action of the application of the ideals of virtue.

This examination of justice is maybe most applicable to the U.S. Constitution. The Constitution, founded on the principle that "We the People" remain the ultimate check and balance of government, demands that even the government must stay under the law. In fact, the first thing established in the Constitution is justice: "We the People ... establish justice."

The Constitution adheres to the natural law as equally as any other aspect of American legal practice:

> We the People, of the United States of America, in order to form a more perfect Union, establish justice, insure domestic tranquility, provide for the common defense, promote the general welfare, and secure the blessings of liberty to ourselves and our posterity. ...

All five promises in the Constitution's preamble are based on one promise: We are *guaranteed* the rights given to each individual through the natural law. No one can escape that this preamble to the Constitution of the United States of America is based on both realist thought (e.g., "the common defense," we must defend what is sacred, such as our rights) and moral thought (e.g., "establish justice," establish what is just and moral in society as the norm).

The belief of the individual that tyranny and the rule of a tyrant is irrationally, irrevocably wrong is also deeply rooted within our Constitution. As was repeatedly noted by the members of the Constitutional Convention, the two things we must be the most wary of in a government are "anarchy and tyranny."[7]

The founders employed logical, historical, and moral arguments against such governments. They discussed a warning note left by the ancient Romans for all future republics to never replace their sacred bond with the people with the platform of an empire. They discussed the innate nature of every individual's freedoms, and they even discussed the logical foundation promoted by the great philosophers that the more power over society given to one government, the more that government has the power to lead the society into destructive ends.

The U.S. Constitution and the rule of law go hand in hand. What's more, the rule of law and *American jurisprudence* go hand in hand.

The rule of law is one of the most crucial underpinnings of all American society. If we do not uphold impartial courts, impartial judicial philosophy, and a view that the Constitution remains the most important cornerstone to our national system, then our republic is in jeopardy, threatened both by anarchy and by tyranny.

FOUR

Conservatives and the Bench

Judicial Philosophy and
the Idea of Strict Constructionism

Judicial Philosophy

While logic and reality with the law is the *factual* conclusions
of any examination of justice and the legal system and the rule
of law is the practical conclusion that it gives us, this does not
mean that they are the *only* conclusions.

Our friends on the left, for example, behave as though there
does not need to be any law but only the word of the government. Such a view is blatantly and utterly naive, but *because
people actually believe in government expansionism,* the left's ideas
on the law must still be considered alternative opinions.

Because it is one out of many such perceptions, the conservative idea of the rule of law becomes itself merely a contending
"opinion" in the grand scheme of things.

Opinions on the law, or "legal philosophy," are often best
seen through the lens of judges. Judges and their opinions on
the law are referred to as *judicial philosophy.*

Of course, this begs a question: How is it possible for a judge
to be impartial, virtuous, and a judicial philosopher at the same
time? How can one both opine on one's feelings about the nature

of law and still expect oneself to be unbiased when confronted with the law as it is presently written? If justice is a virtue and justice is blind, then how is it possible for justice to have an opinion? Wouldn't this take the metaphorical blindfold off justice?

When it comes to the government expansionist, the answer to this would be yes; the blindfold is destroyed by judicial philosophy. Government expansionism is bound to a utopian view that has the end goal of subverting the individual and his or her moral compass to whatever is considered good by the government at the moment. While full destruction of the moral compass is logically impossible, the government expansionist acts as though it is, and continues with a view that morality is not a factor in law. Hence the expansionist is not confined by objectivity to answer legal questions based on the nature of the law itself. The expansionist is free to judge with personal feelings simply by the relative nature of legal positivism.

In conservative jurisprudence, the blindfold remains tightly tied, because conservatives believe in the natural law. If you are confined to logic and to upholding what is right and wrong—and the promotion of what is right—you are confined to the Aristotelian idea that the law looks at both sides without favoritism or partiality, but with a view of "the injury" and *its* relationship to the law.

The Basis of Conservative Legal Philosophy

The conservative legal philosophy, as well as the conservative interpretation of the Constitution, begins with one thing and one thing alone, the rights of the individual.

In order for a government not to become the mammoth entity preferred by government expansionism, the defense must be the average citizen. If the citizen is free, then the government is bound to certain limits on where government ends and where the citizen's rights begin. What's more, in an era in which government expansionism has become a prevalent philosophy for governments around the world, the rights of the people become the only barrier to the government's taking away of any sense of inherent freedom.

The U.S. Constitution clearly states: "No person shall ... be deprived of life, liberty, or property without due process of law." The Constitution means what it says. There are certain rights that cannot be compromised, and there are certain rights that are inherently ours.

All human beings are born as separate entities from any other. And all activities of these human beings are conducted separately from all others.

Freedom is inherent. Realists know this because all reality shows it. Trees do not grow because a human being tells them to grow; they grow because of natural situations. In a similar manner, when children first speak, they do not speak like puppets—that is, not because someone else is doing it for them—they do it *on their own.*

Freedom is like this. Because all human beings are born free and act freely, they naturally must remain free.

Because no reflection on the rule of law can start without a true examination of reality, it is only proper that any philosophical examination of the law through legal philosophy must begin with a strong belief in freedom and individual rights as being naturally and innately given.

It was for the preservation of these rights and freedoms that the founders of our nation wrote the Bill of Rights. The founders believed that a Bill of Rights is necessary to protect the rights of the citizenry from government expansionists. They knew that they were not granting rights to the citizens but merely preserving them so that no government would be able to expand its power over them.

Judicial Activism

Aristotle wrote: "It is not right to pervert the judge by moving him to anger or envy or pity—one might as well warp a carpenter's rule before using it. Again, a litigant has clearly nothing to do but to show that the alleged fact is so or is not so, that it has or has not happened. ... Now, it is of great moment that well-drawn laws should themselves define all the points they possibly can and leave as few as may be to the decision of the judges."[1]

Aristotle's point is not that the courts are invalid, it is that the judge's job is not to make legislative decisions but to interpret the law in the most proper fashion.

The job of the judicial branch of government is to interpret the *current legal status* of the issue at hand, not to write legislation for it. Of course, at different times in history, individuals on the Supreme Court have thought otherwise. These individuals who think that it is the job of the judge to create legislation are called *judicial activists*.

A great example of judicial activism came out of the Proposition 22/Proposition 8 battle in the state of California. On March 7, 2000, the people of California voted for Prop 22, a ban on same-sex marriage.[2] In a state full of leftist Democrats, the vote was certainly a great victory for those who believe in the traditional view of marriage.

It was a great night for many Californians who had prevailed after a long, hard battle, with only six out of the fifty-eight California counties voting *against* the proposition.[3] The numbers were solid as well: 4.6 million Californians in favor and 2.9 million against.[4] Why did Californians show up in such force? The answer is simple: People still believe in the traditional interpretation of marriage. The American people, on the whole, still have traditional values. However, the story continues.

On March 4, 2008, the California Supreme Court heard an appeals case resulting from a three-year legal battle between those who said Proposition 22 was unconstitutional and those who defended its validity.[5] Even though there was, admittedly, "no deeply rooted tradition of same-sex marriage, in the nation or in this state,"[6] the California Supreme Court said in its opinion:

> [We recognize] that the core substantive rights encompassed by the constitutional right to marry apply to same-sex as well as opposite-sex couples.[7]

On May 15, 2008, the court overruled what had been a standing proposition voted on by the people eight years prior.[8]

The moral of the story is not merely that judicial activism is an impediment but that judicial activism is the mute button pressed on the people's voice. If the judiciary becomes all-powerful, then citizens begin to lose their rights and freedoms. In the case of California, the citizens lost the freedom to have their votes counted.

Judicial activism is pushed ardently by many government expansionists. This is for the simple reason that judicial activism gives more power to the government. If the legislative body can't pass a liberal pet project democratically, then it becomes the *court's* responsibility to do so. Moreover, judicial activism, as mentioned, takes away more of the sacred freedoms of the individual, creating the sought-after class warfare.

Judicial activism is often justified in modern America by the writings of former Supreme Court Justice Oliver Wendell Holmes. One of the giants of left-wing political thought, Holmes pioneered new standards for judicial philosophy that would become precedent in the eyes of many. In his magnum opus *The Common Law,* Holmes writes, "The life of the law has not been logic, it has been experience."[9] In this manner, Holmesian legal thought has led the American thinker to the great consequential idea that the law is a manifold beast to be contained only upon the seas of one's emotions and experiential drive; instead of rationalism and reality.

Thus, by embracing Holmesian thought, you divorce yourself from Aristotelian justice—the idea that (as I have noted) the law looks but to the "injury" and not to the "parties"—and engage yourself in a relativistic approach to the law.

Conservative Judicial Philosophy

In opposition to such blatant trampling on the law, conservatives uphold a view of the law—in particular, the Constitution—that states that the judge's job is to merely interpret the law's balance in relation to the law at hand. Moreover, the conservative takes the stance that the law is to be interpreted best in its original philosophy, intent, and literality. Such a view is called *strict constructionism.*

An obvious concern about strict constructionism is what the conservative citizen does when the law at hand is obviously contrary to moral obligation and yet the Constitution is silent on the issue. In instances such as these, the conservative returns to the basics: natural rights. The rights of life, liberty, and property are established as a legal standard in the Constitution. If one of these rights is abridged by the law in question, then the conservative can base a moral argument on the idea that it abridges the individual's rights. Since the individual's inherent rights are themselves moral in that they are in the best interest of humankind, they will never come into conflict with the moral compass.

Take the issue of slavery, for example. In considering how one would judge the U.S. slave laws in their original context, one must first understand slavery for what it is. It is an individual's claim that his right of property can abridge another person's right to liberty. Slavery proves that the rights of multiple individuals cannot be posed against each other without the forfeiture of someone's freedoms. The rights of the individual are constitutionally given to all people inclusively, instead of a few of them exclusively.

The founders believed that the government's job was supposed to be the protection of the people and the people's rights, and they reflected this in the Constitution by dividing the government into three branches, in order to have a system of direct checks and balances.

Maybe the most controversial section of the Constitution is

the Second Amendment, which reads: "A well regulated militia, being necessary to the security of a free state; the right of the people to keep and bear arms shall not be infringed."

Judicial activists often misconstrue this as an outdated amendment to the Constitution. After all, we do not have militias anymore; we have an army. Such people who look at merely the differences between the scenario of today and the scenario of the time in which the law was written are "loose constructionists" because they do not look at the fullness of the philosophical perspective.

This, of course, defies all logic. The amendment does not read "only those in a militia are the people who have the right to keep and bear arms, and for them such shall not be infringed." It reads "the right of the *people* to keep and bear arms shall not be infringed" (emphasis added). Hence, the idea is, once more, inclusive of the whole society, not exclusive to a segment of the society.

Judicial Activism Versus Strict Constructionism

The idea of strict constructionism has, of course, come under intensive direct scrutiny from the "judicial activist" government expansionist.

Robert Scholes of Brown University's Modern Culture and Media Department wrote in a 2007 op-ed piece: "So what can 'strict constructionism' really mean? ... I think it is a coded expression for 'conservative' when used by President Bush, a way of indicating a political position while pretending that judges should be above politics."[10] This is an abomination!

Scholes has missed the entire point of the argument for strict constructionism. Because of the nature of strict construction- ism, the only qualification for believing in it is that you must believe the letter of constitutional law as the strict, rigid found- ing document that it is. Strict constructionism does not cover *all* of conservatism, just as loose constructionism does not cover *all* of government expansionism. It is a *legal philosophy*, not the conservative ideology.

The fact is, strict constructionism does not denote conser- vatism, but conservatism denotes strict constructionism. Strict constructionism is one sector of the conservative ideology that falls into line with the conservative pillars of logic and morality, but many so-called independents and moderates favor strict constructionism. In other words, my argument is simply this: Because of conservatism's views on the rule of law, morality, logic, and history, it is clear that conservatism must be an ide- ology that believes in strict constructionism. But to say that strict constructionism is "a coded expression" for conservatism is absurd. Dr. Scholes, if President Bush had meant he wanted a conservative, he would have said, "I want a conservative!"

Strict constructionism is like many of the other philosophical precedents we have talked about, and will talk about, in this book; it is a key component *of* conservatism, but to say that it *is* conservatism would be fallacious.

Why do I make such a point out of Scholes's statement?

Many in the government expansionist camp adhere to this view and state that strict constructionism is a "coded expres- sion" for "conservative." To say as much not only creates a log- ical fallacy but distracts from the main point. If strict constructionism is conservatism, then we must find another interpretation for the Constitution. If strict constructionism is invalid because it is merely another name for one ideology, then conservatism becomes an ideology without a judicial philosophy. Such important arguments from the opposition must be eagerly addressed.

Of course, government expansionists *hate* strict constructionism. Not only does it oppose judicial activism and loose constructionism, but it also defends individual rights from the impediments of the left, and it harbors, first and foremost, the sacred and inherent rights of every individual.

FIVE

Rights and Independent States

I consider the foundation of the Constitution as laid on this ground: "The powers not delegated to the United States by the Constitution, nor prohibited by it to the States, are reserved to the states respectively, or to the people."

—Thomas Jefferson, *Opinion on National Bank*

The States

In this preceding statement, Jefferson, when quoting the Tenth Amendment, struck a nerve in a manner that we still see today.

The conservative's view on states' rights begins with his belief in realism. Realism teaches that all entities are, because of the natural law, inherently independent of one another. Because such independency exists and is a core aspect of the foundation of conservative thought, it only follows that the individual is, in turn, independent himself.

In an extension of the idea, the inception of our constitutional government—this being a group of states coming *voluntarily* together under one government (just like individuals *voluntarily* coming under government)—makes us believe that the private entities of the states have, just like the individual, a certain sense of independence from the federal government.

Such an idea is part of our national identity. Our nation is the United *States* of America, not the United *Government* of

America. Our nation was not founded like other nations. Unlike the European countries, the United States was not founded on monarchs but on the people, not from the top down but from the bottom up.

Independence

The conservative perspective on states' rights is founded on the same principles as the individual's rights and freedoms; a byproduct of reality and human experience. Independence is differentiated from freedom and liberty in that independence is having no ties to any entity at all, whereas liberty and freedom are merely a distinct breaking of ties between two entities in one specific area. In other words, independence is the completion of freedom and liberty.

Independence is, therefore, the equivalence of self-sovereignty.

Experience has shown us that all individuals are sovereign over themselves, their independence, and their rights. In the same manner, each state—if it is to be truly independent—must be sovereign over its own affairs, free from the meddling hand of the federal government or any other state.

This idea is commonly referred to as *state sovereignty.* In issues directly affecting the states and the freedom of their society, it is best left to the states individually.

The point of state sovereignty is simply this: The more one all-encompassing government is given power, the more government will control society, and the more government controls society, the more the people's inherent and innate rights and freedoms come under fire.

Moreover, I make these comments to clarify the distinction between the terms *states' rights* and *state sovereignty*, because there *is* a distinct difference. States' rights are the inherent and natural facets of the independent states preserved by the action of staying sovereign in their affairs. On the other hand, the action of sovereignty is the independent *station of the state.*

In other words, because of the concept of state sovereignty, we have states' rights. Only independent states can have the ability to exercise power separately from the federal government.

After all, if any independent entity is controlled by another government, then there is no way that the entity can be free to exercise anything *separate from* that government. The logical equation is clear and, to put it in classic syllogistic form: Freedom is part of independence from the government. No part of independence is government dictation, and therefore, freedom is not government dictation. Only if states are separate and independent entities (as ensured by the Tenth Amendment) can the rights of the states be preserved.

The independent and sovereign natures of the states are not to be confused with the idea of one sovereign individual ruling over everything. On the contrary, the term *state sovereignty* is meant to be the opposite of such a sovereign ruler. State sovereignty means that the state is *independent from* the meddling of any other government, while the idea of a sovereign ruler (or ruling body) is meant to be the *engagement in* such meddling.

This is not to say that the states should have all power and the federal government none; what this *is* to say is simply that each state has certain powers that the government has not the liberty nor the *right* to infringe upon. Furthermore, as we will subsequently examine, a federal government has in and of itself a necessary role within governing of the states.

States' Rights Versus Government Expansionism

Naturally, state sovereignty and states' rights are seen as impediments to the government expansionist's endgame. In 2009, Governor Rick Perry of Texas said, "I believe that our federal government has become oppressive in its size, its intrusion into the lives of our citizens, and its interference with the affairs of our state. ... I believe that returning to the letter and spirit of the U.S. Constitution and its essential 10th Amendment will free our state from undue regulations, and ultimately strengthen our Union."[1]

On his MSNBC television program *Countdown,* noted leftist commentator Keith Olbermann called Perry "ignorant" and said that his remarks were advocating "secession."[2] On the same program, *Huffington Post* writer Jim Moore stated that Perry was "trying to stir up his ... radical fringe to get them excited about him as governor."[3] Olbermann and the rest of the mainstream media were not tweaked by the governor because of his comments alone, but because he was dislodging the cornerstone of government expansionist philosophy: the expansion of the size and scope of government.

While the left was genuinely angry, the cry of secessionism was utterly bogus, an attack made up of politically expedient arguments meant to hurt the governor's reputation. Perry was not a secessionist; he was just a conservative whose goal was to preserve the Tenth Amendment and the sovereignty of the independent states.

Secessionists are in a much different boat from conservatives; in fact, they don't even board at the same dock! Secessionists deny the federal government any constitutional viability whatsoever. Conservatives who support states' rights claim that the federal government has complete viability, but that the states have a certain set of constitutional powers that the federal government has no right to touch.

Lesson learned: In the mind of the government expansionist, you either fall complacently and completely in line with the federal government's demands, or you are deemed a hardcore secessionist.

The left applies "secessionism" as a cover. The *true* dissension between conservatism and expansionism on states' rights is found on the issue of the federal government's size and scope.

The left tars the conservative movement with the label of "secessionists" because it is an easy way to divert the citizenry's attention from the government expansionist's dystopia and create suspicion that conservatives want to divide the nation. It is a dishonest and morally reprehensible ploy on the part of the left.

The left's view of states as entities that ought to heed the federal government's beck and call is totally absurd. If states are independent entities, then they deserve to be treated as such, not as dependent entities.

The right sees this relationship differently. The power of the state includes everything not set aside explicitly by the constitution as a federal power. The conservative believes that the state, as an independent entity, has clear boundaries differentiating it from the federal government. The purpose of the Tenth Amendment, to the conservative, is to acknowledge the independent nature of the states and to give credence to states' power.

The rights of the states derived from their sovereignty and independence is ever so important. If the states do not have freedom from the federal government, then they easily become subsidiaries *of* the federal government. The Tenth Amendment is as important as the First Amendment and must be upheld if one cares about the integrity and strict constructionist interpretation of the Constitution. States' rights, though often ignored, must be respected. It is the key to securing boundaries on government in America.

SIX

On Governmental Boundaries

Introduction

The preamble to the U.S. Constitution reads: "We the People of the United States of America, in order to form a more perfect Union, establish Justice, insure domestic tranquility, provide for the common Defense, promote the general Welfare, and preserve the blessings of Liberty to ourselves and our posterity."

Of course, the preamble presents the thesis of the Constitution, which includes the words "form," "establish," "insure," "provide," "promote," and "preserve." It does not once mention "help," "bailout," "institutionalize," or "run" any aspect of America.

The left interprets the term "promote the general Welfare" to mean "provide people with welfare checks." And as government expansionists, leftists interpret the entire preamble as a warrant for the federal government to regulate "We the People."

If ever there were a need to clarify the foundational ideas behind the federal government in the Constitution, it is now.

We find government expansionists who, every day, wait to find a new loophole or a new opportunity to create more new power for themselves. New regulations are dreamed up, new taxes are proposed, and new policies are established by the left and affect the daily life of every individual. The fact is, our Constitution never established and cannot establish a government that pivots on the whim of a politician, *but a society that pivots* on the structured nature of the document itself.

Constitutional Boundaries and Justice

Because our society is based on the Constitution and the rule of law in general, the question must naturally arise, how is it that we keep this society structured this way?

The answer is simple. The only way to uphold *any* structure in society is through justice and the rule of law. If justice is not real but merely an opinion, and if reality is only an arrangement based upon our personal opinions, then we live in a fake matrix with no moral absolutes, no logical conclusions, no necessity for punishment, no truth, and therefore no necessity to act in a "good" manner. What's more, if there is no rule of law, then we mustn't fret about people disobeying the Constitution. The absence of justice creates a society without boundaries for anything, the absence of reality means no moral boundaries, and the absence of reality means no more common sense.

But, as previous chapters of this book have endeavored to prove, these things do exist.

Justice is just as real as my own right eye. And reality is as natural as the tree in the forest. Nothing is fallacious about the rule of law; the only thing fallacious within it is the denial thereof!

The validity of constitutional boundaries on the government follows from the validity of justice and the rule of law. Because justice is based on the difference between right and wrong and upholding the right in society—thereby making the phrase "establish justice" in the Constitution the logical equivalent of "establish virtue"—it only makes sense that to have a "good" or "virtuous" government, we must first have a government rooted in justice and the rule of law. In other words, if we are to have a good and virtuous federal government, then it too must be rooted in the confines of the rule of law and justice.

Our Constitution defines the practices of government. Of course, in defining what a government *can* do, one is simultaneously defining what government *cannot* do. By saying that certain things are the *only* things an entity can do, you are in turn saying that everything else falls into the category of things the entity *cannot* do.

Moreover, if government is able to do *anything* it wants—as legal positivism suggests—this defeats the purpose of having a rule of law or, much less, a Constitution! If a government is able to do anything, then it becomes immune from justice and is only confined by its own ideas of right and wrong.

What's more, if this occurs, the federal government destroys the values of justice. By destroying boundary lines, the federal government establishes its own standards, thereby denying any credence owed to the moral compass and logic.[1]

Specifics on Governmental Boundaries

At a meeting of the Chicago Executives' Club in 1975, Ronald Reagan spoke about government expansionism:

> This absorption of revenue by all levels of government, the
> alarming rate of inflation and the rising toll of unemployment

all stem from a single source: the belief that government, particularly the federal government, has the answer to our ills, and that the proper method of dealing with social problems is [to] transfer power from the private to the public sector, and within the public sector from the state and local governments to the central government in Washington.[2]

Reagan here leaves us with a serious philosophical enigma: Where must government's power end?

The Fifth Amendment of the U.S. Constitution clearly states: "No person ... shall be deprived of life, liberty, or property, without due process of law. ..." This denotes that no governmental bureaucracy, nor any government bureaucrat, can have limitless authority.

Let me begin by giving an example of blurred government boundaries and the havoc they wreak. This one deals with commerce authority.

One small statement in the Constitution known as the "commerce clause" (a.k.a. Article 1, Section 8, Clause 3) gives Congress the stated ability "to regulate commerce with foreign nations, and among the several states, and with the Indian tribes."

The term "regulate" is, of course, a toxic term in today's political climate. Government expansionists jump with glee at the idea of regulation almost as joyfully as they jump at the idea of spending. And freedom-driven individuals cringe as much at the idea almost as much as they cringe at the idea of the abridgment of their rights.

Commerce is not something to be dealt with lightly. In 1936, the Supreme Court heard the case of *United States v. Butler*, in which the question was the viability of the Agriculture Adjustment Act of 1935. This act heavily regulated and taxed farmers in order to "establish and maintain such balance between the production and consumption of agricultural commodities, and such marketing conditions therefore, as will reestablish prices to farmers at a level that will give agricultural commodities a purchasing power with respect to articles that farmers buy equivalent to the purchasing power of agricultural commodities in the base period."[3] As one can see, the bill's simple goal was to regulate the farming industry.

Because of its obvious intent on regulating the agriculture industry, this act was overturned by the Supreme Court. The Court's opinion reads: "The act invades the reserved rights of the states. It is a statutory plan to regulate and control agricultural production, a matter beyond the powers delegated to the federal government. The tax, the appropriation of the funds raised, and the direction for their disbursement are parts of the plan. They are but means to an unconstitutional end."[4]

The Constitution gave the government the ability "to regulate commerce ... among the several states" but not to regulate commerce *within* the states. This case shows a defining line between the powers of the federal government and the state government.

The federal government is given the ability to regulate any commerce occurring between two states ("trade, traffic, or transportation" that moves between two of the independent states in our nation), international commerce (commerce between the United States, or any of the independent states, and a foreign power), and Native American commerce (commerce between the nation and Native American tribes).[5]

Under the Tenth Amendment, any other regulation must be left to the states. And because the basic action of farm production and cultivation—as discussed in this case—happens as "a purely local activity," it only follows that the states, and not the federal government, have the right and power to define the laws concerning such activity.[6]

The question then becomes, what if an individual or a large agricultural company were to—for example—drain a river that crosses state lines? Is that, too, "a purely local activity"?[7] First, one must recognize this question—though a valid one—as a different question than that addressed in *Butler*. In his opinion on the case, Justice Roberts writes of the question being addressed: "The third clause endows the Congress with power 'to regulate Commerce ... among the several States.' Despite a reference in its first section to a burden upon, and an obstruction of the normal currents of commerce, the act under review does not purport to regulate transaction in interstate or foreign commerce."[8] In this manner, the Justice has given credence to two things: (1) that if the issues at hand were to be a physical activity that cultivates or farms land in a manner such as the aforementioned interstate farming example, then—yes—that is a question to be applied to federal activity and (2) that the question made during the *Butler* case was, however, not such a question, and therefore, federal power under the commerce clause does not apply here.

The point is simply this: The federal government has certain boundaries that cannot be ignored. The commerce clause, as seen here, exemplifies how the ideas proposed in the Constitution for the federal government are supposed to be lines beyond which the government should not cross. Moreover, the Tenth

Amendment teaches us that certain powers delegated to the states are prohibited from the reach of the federal government.

But the issue goes deeper still. The Constitution is written in very specific terms. From each individual article down to each individual clause, we find specific guidelines for the practices of government:

> Congress shall have the power to lay and collect taxes, duties, imposts and excises, to pay the debts and provide for the common defense and general welfare of the United States; but all duties, imposts, and excises shall be uniform throughout the United States. (Article 1, Section 8, Clause 1)

> [Congress shall have the authority] To borrow money on the credit of the United States. ... (Article 1, Section 8, Clause 2)

> [Congress shall have the authority] To coin money, regulate the value thereof, and of foreign coin, and fix the standard of weights and measures. ... (Article 1, Section 8, Clause 5)

These are just a few excerpts of the Constitution. The principle of each clause, each sentence, and each phrase of the U.S. Constitution is thus: The federal government has the authority to do the said action, but it does not have the authority to do any action not delegated to it. Thus, the Constitution serves as both a boundary around and an outline for government in general.

The left behaves as though the federal government has authority beyond what's delegated to it. *They believe* that the Constitution is a valid document, but that it must be changed to fit the evolving needs of government. They believe that the Constitution is a "living document" and that it is too outdated for proper use today.

While the left might consider the Constitution a collection of guidelines for government—guidelines that can be tweaked or disregarded—the conservative sees the Constitution as the definitive boundary and power-giver for the federal government.

The Constitution is not a living document. It fits our needs today just as much as it fit the needs of the founders. While the times may change, principles are *timeless*. The philosophical principle that a government with too much power is a threat to society, inherent rights, and liberty is equally as applicable today as it was more than two hundred years ago. What's more, boundaries defending a society *against* such a government have the same logical and moral validity as they did in any previous era.

BOOK THREE

Human Life

SEVEN

What Is Life?

In the summer of 1822, the poet Percy Bysshe Shelley worked on what would be his final poem, *The Triumph of Life*. With some of the last strokes of his pen, Shelley wrote his ultimate question, "Then, what is life?"[1] We have had more than 185 years to ponder this question, but it still remains unanswered in many people's minds.

The question may seem silly in the mind of the modern reader, who might brush off this question with a little laughter and a lot of sarcasm.

But defining what we mean by the word *life* is intrinsically important to understanding it. In modern times, the idea of defining terms before using them has been ignored, and in turn, words, concepts, and whole phrases have become increasingly ambiguous.

Many people think of life as simply the time during which they inhabit the earth, and this is not untrue.

Georg Hegel—the widely recognized father of Marxian thought—wrote a definition of *life* in his work *Encyclopedia of Philosophical Sciences:* "Life is essentially something alive." In this manner, the term *life* in Hegelian thought becomes simply a thought pattern based upon the state of one's existence. It is in following this line of thought that the leftist mind-set in the twenty-first century concludes that life is only one's time alive, or in other words, life is merely a state of being.

This term, *state of being,* pivots on its opportune word: *being.* The term *being* refers to the idea of existence, which denotes a state of movement, action, or function. As only those things considered living by the common man can actually and naturally engage in these actions, it seems only fitting that the idea of a state of being (i.e., a state of existence) be connected to the idea of life.

Unlike those on the left, however, who define life in a mere material sense, conservatives define life as its essence. The conservative views life not as a time period or a state of being, but as an inherent right of humans. In other words, it is a property of reality.

Reality and experience teach us that our rights are not things government or society can give to us, but they are things every human being is inherently given and entitled to by a Creator. It was this idea that the founders applied to life when they wrote in the Declaration of Independence that all men "are endowed by their Creator with certain inalienable rights, that among them are Life, Liberty, and the pursuit of Happiness."

The idea of life as an "inalienable right" is best understood in contrast to the idea of what life would be as an "alienable right."

Inalienable rights are those that cannot be taken away, while alienable rights *can* be separated from the person, or seized. Of course, the facts have shown us that all rights of the individual are inherent and unassailable. Reality and logic have taught us that we are born free, and we naturally want to live free and with certain inherent rights. We are born with rights; they are never given to us.

Of course, if no person or government gives us our rights in the first place, by what authority does anyone have the ability to take away our rights? If they are inherently *ours,* it denotes that they are inherently *no one else's.* In other words, if our rights are inherent, then they must be inalienable at the same time; after all, if they are alienable, then that defeats the entire purpose of our rights being inherently our rights and our rights alone.

An understanding of inalienable rights is best gained through the lens of a logical argument: All natural rights are inalienable and inherent; therefore, no rights are alienable and given. Therefore, the notion of alienable rights is an oxymoron.

Thus, the question must be asked: What is the conservative's opinion on an issue such as the death penalty? After all, would not taking an individual's life via legal procedure be itself a violation of the individual's right to *life?*

John Locke maybe summed it up best: "[The capital criminal] has forfeited his own life."

In other words, in the commitment of a crime of a certain severity, an individual has given his or her liberty and freedom to justice and must be punished with severity in line with the crime. Therefore, to deny a murderer the right of life is not to break with natural law, but merely to punish the person in accordance with the natural law.

The Purpose of Life

Now that we understand the definition of life, we can answer this second question: What is the purpose of life?

While this may seem like an unimportant inquiry in the grand scheme of things, it isn't. The conservative's belief in the life is simply based and rooted in a belief in the moral compass.

If there is a good and a bad, and a right and a wrong, then the conservative—who is a logical realist—must align with what is good and right.

As Aristotle said, "Every art and every inquiry, and similarly every action and pursuit, is thought to aim at some good; and for this reason the good has rightly been declared to be that at which all things aim."[2] The conservative believes that it should be the drive of the individual to strive for what is right and what is good. The moral compass gives *purpose* to the idea of life as a right.

In fact, if there is no moral compass, then we are denied the logical ability to say that life is an inalienable right. If there is no good, then there is no standard for what can and cannot be taken away from us.

The purpose of life, in the conservative's mind, is to do what is just (i.e., what is virtuous), whatever is good, and whatever is in accordance with the inherent moral compass.

Moreover, the conservative's view on the purpose of life goes deeper. If life is a *right* of humankind, then it only makes sense that the individual act on it. In other words, by the nature of a right, the person is more or less *compelled* to live.

The government expansionist, however, looks at things in a completely different light from the conservative. An expansionist's idea of life as merely *existence* and *being* implies that the purpose of life is merely to exist and to be. In other words, the purpose of life is merely to live. But what must we do while we are living? Such an idea does not answer this question for the individual. This begs the question, how do we fill this void?

If our purpose is merely to exist, the left explains, then the rest of society's aspects will be filled by the government, in the expansionist's "nanny" state. The government will take care of you, the poor, pitiful human being. All you have to do is exist, and the government will do everything else.

The government expansionist turns the independent sovereignty of the life of the individual into the dependent station of governmental institutionalization.

The Value of Life

But there is still one more question that begs to be answered: What is the *value* of life?

By saying that life is something that is "endowed [to individuals] by their Creator," we are giving life a position at the top of our priority list. If life is inherent, if God endows it, and if it is inalienable, then the value of life is ineffably high.

On the other hand, if we are merely here to exist or to be and if there is no real purpose for living except for ... well ... living, then it only follows that life has a small value. What's more, the left couples such mere existence with its denial of the moral compass. If there is no moral compass, then we have no standard for the value of human life.

Human life becomes the equivalent of the life of an animal or a tree, and for this reason, the rights of the animal approach the equivalent of the rights of the individual in the minds of those on the left. In a similar manner, the left turns the definition of life of the individual, since it is merely existence, into the equivalent of the life of a tree, since it too exists. With this as the left's value for life, the government expansionist philosophy meets its ugly stepchildren: animal rights groups such as PETA and environmental groups like the Earth Liberation Front.

It may seem odd to the logically thinking conservative that the government expansionists would say that we need to "save the animals" and "save the trees" with the same fervor and with the same value for life that they give to the human being, but it is not odd to the government expansionist! After all, since ignoring the moral compass leads to a society without boundaries, then the left is free to define its own standards any way that it sees fit. This is not because the government expansionist believes in some different moral code (after all, there is only one moral code), but simply because the left denies the one moral code that does exist and replaces it with a Holmesian/Hegelian view touched with a mix of Hobbes' mechanism.

The left cannot say that it believes in a different morality than we do, because there is only one morality. The only thing the left can answer is whether it denies morality and life wholeheartedly, or embraces it.

EIGHT

Views and Values

Life Is Universal

Before we continue with this discussion of conservatism, let me draw up some important observations from the idea that life is an inherent right.

First, the conservative's belief in life as an inherent right must be seen in the most universal sense. The conservative believes that all rights are natural and, therefore, any right must be understood as a fact of all society rather than a gift *from* society. In other words, life is not something for one section of society; it is an inherent right of all humans, something we are born with. Just as the human being is born free and wants to continue to *be free,* the human being is born with life and naturally *wants to live.*

The philosophical principle is thus: that every individual has the right to live, and that this right is something no government or other human being has the right to take away or infringe on.

Under the philosophical principle underscored here, that life is an inherent and inalienable right, no individual should be valued at a higher price than others.

It is this impediment that government expansionists often encounter when they come out with universal health-care legislation. Some people cost more to care for than others, so it may be that we have to "value" certain lives over other lives to save money ... so says the government expansionist. Columnist Evan Thomas wrote in the *Newsweek* cover article "The Case for Killing Granny," "the need to spend less money on the elderly at the end of life is the elephant in the room in the health-reform debate. Everyone sees it but no one wants to talk about it. At a more basic level, Americans are afraid not just of dying, but of talking and thinking about death. Until Americans learn to contemplate death as more than a scientific challenge to be overcome, our health-care system will remain unfixable."[1] In other words, we find an editor at large of a major news magazine proclaiming as his thesis that Americans need to *get over death!* Forget the moral and ethical questions of "Killing Granny," and instead embrace an approach that says we must find "treatments to cut out," and succinctly cut them, for the simple reason of saving money.[2]

The conservative chafes at this idea and asks the government expansionist, Which is worth more, life or money? It seems quite unethical for us to value the life of an individual according to economic factors. Only through moral and legal relativism may an individual bend morality to be a set of standards that are only so applicable as they meet your political agenda.

But such impediments as morality and ethics mean nothing to the government expansionist if they are in the way of his or her goal of increasing governmental power. Therefore, while it may not make sense to the sensible, it makes perfect sense to the left!

"Do What Is Right and Not What Is Wrong"

The conservative understands life not only as an innate, universal, natural, and inalienable right but also as something that must have the end goal of doing what is right and, therefore, not what is wrong. This may seem all too obvious for discussion, but it is quite important.

By saying it in both formats, "Do what is right," and "Do not what is wrong," we highlight two separate functions of the same idea. The first merely says act according to the moral compass, which is, as previously discussed, the conservative's understanding of the purpose of life. "Do not what is wrong" means do *not* those things that go *against* the moral compass. The key is not to understand the two expressions as separate goals but as the same one. Again, "Do what is right while not doing what is wrong." Of course, as humans we will sometimes fail in that endeavor, but that is not the point. We must strive to do only the right things and to avoid all immoral things.

Of course, we are often confronted with necessary evils. In the nature of war, for instance, we find it necessary to engage in bloodshed for the simple reason of defending our nation. Thus, there is a certain importance in recognizing such necessary evils.

The Value of the Individual in General

If life as a *right* is more valuable than the notion of life as a *state of being*, then it only follows that individuals, whose life is seen as a right, are valued more than individuals under the government expansionist precept, who merely exist.

If life, being the most essential aspect of humanity, is valued highly, then the living individual will, in turn, be valued highly. What's more, if life is valued *less* highly, then the living individual will necessarily be seen "less highly" as well.

Discussion of valuing life more or less highly refers to a scale standard of high and low based on the inherent moral compass's standard of right and wrong. Because the left denies this moral compass, there is really no such scale for the left, and therefore, they can claim they value life as highly as anyone. Once more, the denial of the moral compass frees expansionists to say whatever they want and to define their own standard.

By valuing the individual according to standards—as the conservative does—it becomes apparent that the natural independence of the individual is affirmed. In sum, the properties of life itself denote three all-important facts:

1. The right of life is *universal.*
2. The purpose of life is best stated as not merely "Do what is right," but also "Do what is right while not doing what is wrong."
3. The individual is valued highly under the idea that life is a right, while he or she is valued less highly under the idea that life is a state of being.

It is important to understand these three aspects of life if one wants to understand the entirety of the life issue. The fact is, we often overlook philosophical tenants such as these in exchange for policy. It is the philosophy that *sustains* the policy.

NINE

When Does Life Begin?

And Other Issues on the Right of the Individual to Have Life

The Personhood Question

If life is a universal entity, if it is an inherent right, and if it is something that must be valued highly, then the obvious question is, when does life begin?

First, if life is universal and if it is inalienable, it is important to understand when life begins.

To answer this question, one must keep in mind that the transitions from embryo to fetus to the birth of a child are not described by scientists as a series of shifts from nonhuman into human, but are considered stages of development.[1] To say that a certain stage of development is less "human" than another stage would be illogical and wrong.

We know that a living entity cannot be generated from an inanimate object. Scientists once believed this was possible, but the theory of spontaneous generation was proven false in the 1700s and 1800s. Now we know that a piece of moldy cheese and a rag in a kitchen corner *attract rats;* however, they are not responsible for the rats' creation. And a piece of meat attracts flies, but does not create maggots. And yet leftists will preposterously claim the logical equivalent that the embryo and fetus can be nonhuman, while the subsequent newborn infant can be human. Like the spontaneous-generation theory about rats and worms, the left's theory on when one becomes a human being states that one entity can give genesis to a completely different entity.

If nonhuman and human were stages of the same process, any person with an underdeveloped brain, or a nondeveloped limb, or an underdeveloped organ would be "less human" than fully developed people. Do we really believe that human development denotes a difference between human and nonhuman?

Adolf Hitler's persecution of the infirm throughout the Holocaust is well documented. The fascist-Marxist left in Germany at the time felt it was permissible to kill, maim, and even *experiment* on the underdeveloped because they were believed to be less than human. Is this the standard of our society?

No, of course it isn't. We do not believe this to be correct any more than we believe murder to be correct.

My point is simple: The human embryo and fetus must, by logical deduction, be a *human being* just as much as a newborn child *outside the womb* is. Therefore, human life begins at conception. The conceived child is entitled to the same rights as any other human.

To Change a People, and How to Fix Their Minds on Something Other Than Morality

The left is vexed by the things that Karl Marx referred to as "religious ... illusions."[2] These so-called illusions are the morals that have become a part of our own personal thoughts and individual standards. The leftist finds his or her agenda endangered when the individual is blinded by these "illusions."[3]

Of course, the leftist will want to explain away these illusions and create *disillusions* in their place—disillusions that will naturally lead to opportunities for government expansionism. Therefore, the leftist seeks to cast doubt on morality and rationality. If neither is seen as absolutely certain, then conservatism, which is based on these two—along with history—becomes itself incorrect. Moreover, because the left is based on the denial of these two, the left begins itself to be seen as *correct!*

In determining personhood and defining life, the left sets up the disillusion—by its own standard, of course—that human life *does not* begin at conception. Any life before birth is itself merely an aspect of the *mother's* life, and the entity within the womb has no rights but those granted by the mother's discretion.

I will not analyze the obvious logical fallacies enmeshed in this thinking, because it is overly relativistic and thereby so riddled with lapses of logic that it is meaningless. But I do grant that the leftist, by dispelling a religious people's "illusions" and offering purported enlightenment on the issue of "personhood," obliterates reality when arguing that abortion is permissible.

The "Inconvenient" Pregnancy

I do not believe that anyone on the left honestly *wants* to have the abortion procedure administered. However, the left *does not care* whether abortion is administered, because they argue it is not immoral. They are supportive of the procedure because they deny life its inherency, and they are apathetic about the actual life and death issues that abortion entails because they deny, and want to destroy, the "religious ... illusions" of the moral compass. It is not the murder of a *human being* but the "termination" of a *nonhuman* entity, such as a tumor.

Because of the moral compass, conservatives must find themselves estranged from abortion at all stages. If human life, or personhood, begins at conception, and if, at the same time, abortion is right but murder is wrong, then the conservative in support of abortion becomes caught in a logical dilemma. If the conservative simply embraces abortion, but not murder, then he or she is denying the universality of the moral compass's jurisdiction over all human beings.

At the same time many on the left feel that the inconvenience of an unwanted pregnancy trumps the moral debate of whether abortion is right or wrong. Whether it's financial circumstances or a less-than-ideal family life, a person facing an unwanted pregnancy can always count on the left's defense of abortion. Few on the left stop to consider the inconvenience that death causes the unborn human or the convenience that the life-honoring institution of adoption might provide all parties.

Because the left denies the moral compass and creates its *own* standard for society in its stead, the government expansionist can advocate abortion by claiming it eliminates "inconveniences" for women by destroying an innocent child's life. In the same breath, however, the leftist can claim that a hardened criminal (and a threat to society) does not deserve the death penalty. This is because expansionists create their own standards as they go along.

States' Rights and Life

However important the conservative believes the protection of life is, conservatism emphasizes that the issue is not charged to the federal government. As a strict constructionist with a strong respect for states' rights, the conservative believes in the principle of federalism; thus the conservative believes that the issue of abortion belongs to the states and the people to decide because the Constitution does not mention life as an issue on which the federal government must rule.

Though abortion wasn't a major issue during the era in which the Constitution was written, the principles of federalism, states' rights, and strict constructionism still apply. The 1973 United States Supreme Court case of *Roe v. Wade,* considered by many to be very shoddy jurisprudence, robbed states of their right to regulate or outlaw abortion.

"Jane Roe" brought a suit to the U.S. Supreme Court against the constitutionality of Texas's state criminal abortion law, and the Court ruled: "State criminal abortion laws, like those involved here, that except from criminality only a life-saving procedure on the mother's behalf without regard to the stage of her pregnancy and other interests involved violate the Due Process Clause of the Fourteenth Amendment, which protects against state action the right to privacy, including a woman's qualified right to terminate her pregnancy."[4]

First, clearly the Supreme Court missed the point that "to terminate her pregnancy" a woman must "terminate" her baby, a living human being. But aside from the Court's blatant defense of abortion, there are serious constitutional flaws in the Supreme Court's argument.

One of those flaws is that the Constitution's so-called "right to privacy" is not applicable to abortion in the manner that Justice Harry Blackmun claims it is. The "right to privacy" is an implied right, given via Constitution by an express guarantee to "liberty." The "right to privacy" is the idea that because we have a right to act on our own accord, we have a right to do so free from anyone else's action or prying eye. This is a logical and real conclusion.

However, such action is limited. If you are acting in a manner that comes into conflict with the law, then you have stepped out of your private affairs. In this case, your affairs are between yourself and the law.

Furthermore, if your actions affect another that, too, is no longer your "private" affair. In such a case, your affairs now become those of yourself and all those affected.

Finally, if you act in a manner that harms another individual, a group of individuals, or the whole society, you have overstepped the boundaries of your liberty, because by *harming* another you infringe upon *their* equally inherent right to privacy and security. This is as John Locke wrote in his *Second Treatise on Government;* "no one ought to harm another in his life, health, liberty, or possessions. ..."

Thus if we can conclude philosophically that the unborn child has a right to life—something that we have already concluded—then it would be an abridgement of logic and fact to conclude that an individual's right to privacy can supersede another individual's right to life.

The Fourteenth Amendment's "Due Process Clause," mentioned in the argument for *Roe v. Wade,* says: "No state shall make or enforce any law which shall abridge the privileges or immunities of citizens of the United States; nor shall any state deprive any person of life, liberty, or property, without due process of law." If Roe's right to privacy and liberty was infringed by the Texas law, then what about the child's right to life? No, when the founders discussed liberty, they never intended it to mean that you would try to protect someone's "conveniences" while denying someone else's life. The founders believed that all three—life, liberty, and property—must be *harmonious* in society.

Conservatives believe that *Roe v. Wade* must be overturned, not merely because of the belief that life begins at conception, but also because the conservative believes that the issue of abortion should be one decided by the states and the people, not the federal government.

The reasoning used to prove the sacred and inherent nature of life must be applied to the debate within the states, and the constitutional argument for natural rights must apply *legally* in the states just as much as it is applied to the whole of society.

Because all individuals are constitutionally guaranteed their right to life, to write legislation contrary to this would be to violate the *agreement among the States* and thereby violate what is—in application—universal law for all aspects of society.

BOOK FOUR

Limited Government

TEN

A Private and Public Sector

And the Necessity Thereof

**Limited Government as Naturally Created:
An Introduction to the Private and Public Sectors**

If there are two things that the conservative takes prides in more than anything else, they would be the protection of the individual and his or her rights and freedoms and, second, the preservation of government within its most limited format. To understand these as separate classifications of the conservative's view on society would be incorrect; they must be understood as they are, interconnected inasmuch as the first denotes the second.

The conservative believes that the rights of the individual are inherently necessary to the person's physical security and his or her own personal sovereignty. Because conservatives believe that these rights are of such importance, they conclude that the protection of these rights must be priority number one. In asserting one priority over another, one acknowledges that the higher priority occupies a closer standing to what is most good morally. And in upholding the rights of the individual as the top priority, the conservative recognizes the innate and inherent rights of the individual as being very close to the core of the moral compass.

Because the rights of the individual are inalienable, important, and unable to be taken away or destroyed by anyone, a natural boundary is drawn between the power of outside sources and the power, or sovereign rights, of the individual. It is this boundary that defines the basis of a limited government.

But to say this has several implications. If the government is supposed to be limited in its size and scope, then it only follows that those things protected and preserved by our natural rights for the sovereign and independent individual are separate in jurisdiction from those of the government, for if the two were identical in jurisdiction, then their size and scope would be identical as well. In such a hypothetical situation, the government would become *unlimited*, thereby creating a society in which human rights are disrespected. A limited government is an implication of our inherent rights and freedoms, and logically, a *large government* is the by-product of the denial of the inherent rights and freedoms of the individual.

This idea of a limited government and its relationship to the natural boundaries created and inferred by the natural rights and freedoms of the individual creates a pronounced delineation between the individual and government. It stipulates a government sector and a civilian sector, or the public sector and the private sector.

In order to understand the limitations of government, one must understand the differences between the two.

The Private and Public Sector on Wealth Creation

First, the private sector is the domain of the producer and consumer. Wealth, after all, is not merely the product, but also the result of production. As Adam Smith defined it in his classic *The Wealth of Nations,* "real wealth ... [is] the annual produce of the land and labour of the society."[1]

The classical definition of this kind of wealth—or "real wealth," as Smith called it—is not merely a coin, metal, or paper currency, but the *production* that achieves the result of that coin, metal, or other piece of currency.

The private sector is the sector of the producer, and the creation of wealth is an extension of the people's *right* to a "pursuit of happiness." *Pursuit of* is different from *achievement of,* in that the individual *pursues* something to reach the *achievement.*

Achievement is the goal of the pursuance, and in this case, the goal of the pursuit of happiness is material wealth. In other words, because this pursuit is found to be the right of the *private independent sovereign,* it only follows that the individual in the private sector has the sole ability to produce wealth.

It is not the right of the public sector. Moreover, this right to the creation of wealth must remain an aspect of only the private sector because the individual is, and must remain, naturally *independent* of government.

If government becomes the creator of wealth, then a dependency of the individual on a sector of the government develops. It is impossible for an individual to compete with the government, since government can tacitly threaten every individual's freedom and life, while the citizen *cannot.*

Accordingly, a government-run economy cannot coexist with a private-sector-run economy. In the case of economics, there is hardly any gray area in this matter.

However, there is a strong necessity for regulatory practices. Just as much as law is necessary, government is necessary to uphold the law. To regulate society in pursuit of both the common good of humanity and the preservation of stability is both reasonable and necessary; however, such regulations must be carefully measured in relation to their effects upon the people and their rights.

Furthermore, it must be duly noted that the *constitutional* authority of our federal government under the regulatory aspect of the commerce clause is *real,* and for this matter, we might say that in American economics, *pure laissez-faire* is not reasonable, seeing as *pure laissez-faire* is the absence of regulation whatsoever.

Property Rights and the Two Sectors

This brings me to my second point about the private sector; the private sector is the sector of property. Property, in most cases, must be individually owned—not publically owned. What's more, that which is individually owned must not be taken from the private sector and awarded to the public sector. The public-use clause of the Fifth Amendment states: "No person shall ... be deprived of life, liberty, or property, without due process of law; nor shall private property be taken for public use, without just compensation."

The principle for this right of "private property" is quite simple, really. If the individual is free and independent, then those things that he or she owns individually ("property") must naturally be regarded as a part of the individual in the calculation of the person's material worth. Therefore, since such property is a part of a person's material worth, it only follows that such property becomes independent, as the person is. In this manner, property becomes a station of our natural rights and freedoms.

One of the greatest debates and discussions on private property rights stems from *Kelo v. City of New London,* heard by the U.S. Supreme Court in 2005. In this case, the Connecticut city of New London was accused of violating the public-use clause of the Fifth Amendment by forcing individuals to forfeit their property to the city, whose government wished to award it to *another* private party.

The court ruled in favor of the city, and the majority opinion, as written by then-Justice Stevens, said:

> In 2000, the city of New London approved a development plan that, in the words of the Supreme Court of Connecticut, was "projected to create in excess of 1,000 jobs, to increase tax and other revenues, and to revitalize an economically distressed city, including its downtown and waterfront areas." ... In assembling the land needed for this project, the city's development agent has purchased property from willing sellers and proposes to use the power of eminent domain to acquire the remainder of the property from unwilling owners in exchange for just compensation, ... Because that plan unquestioningly serves a public purpose, the takings challenged here satisfy the public use requirement of the Fifth Amendment.[2]

There is one complete fallacy in Justice Stevens's thesis, however.

One must note the rickety skeleton of eminent domain, as it has been interpreted. A modern interpretation of eminent domain begins with the idea that the taking of your property to promote the public interest is okay, even if done by force to individuals resisting. Eminent-domain abusers read the Fifth

Amendment's words "nor shall private property be taken for public use, without just compensation" and interpret this as simply saying that if the individual's property is (a) wanted for a public use and (b) justly compensated for, then everything is fine. But what if the individual refuses to give up the land, even after the two aspects of the public-use clause have been satisfied? Eminent-domain abusers—who are generally government expansionists—say the individual must *still* give up the land to the government. The promoters of this view are wrong, not because eminent domain *is wrong* but because these people see property as merely an object of governmental opportunity instead of a tool for the help of the public (as it was meant to be treated).

By insisting on "just compensation" for individuals, our nation's founders meant for the Fifth Amendment to guarantee that eminent domain would be an *exchange* of wealth, not an occupation of rights. My opinion, in this sense, is simply that when the government treats eminent domain based upon the opinion in Kelo, we find a flawed status quo that seems to state that the right of the individual to his property is only as real *as the government allows it to be.*

The idea of eminent domain itself smacks of good intentions, to do what is in the interest of the public on the whole; it is, however, the *principle* and the idea of eminent domain that are harmful. Property is a right of the individual, and it is best left in the hands of the private sector.

Freedom and the Two Sectors

The private sector is the sector of freedom of speech, press, and religion. In all actuality, it might be more accurately stated that the idea of *being* free and the idea of freedom in general are best seen within the context of the private sector. It only makes sense that something such as my freedom to speak, to write, and to believe that which I want to believe is a unique characteristic that the individual is given in the facts of nature and in the facts of his independence. If something is to be a right of the citizen and, individually, of the whole of society, then it must not be something dictated and controlled by a body of individuals, such as the government. Public sector rule of freedom would turn freedom around.

If the individual's freedoms are by nature a facet of the sovereign human being, and if, at the same time, a governing body decides that these same freedoms come under its control, then such individual freedoms cannot be truly termed freedoms, but government grants. If government controls my right to speak freely, for example, then I am not truly going to ever speak freely but speak only on the terms granted by the government. (Of course, if our rights are natural, then, once more, the government will never be able to truly take away our freedoms, but rather punish us by threatened force for exercising them.)

Freedom itself, being natural and innate to the individual, becomes itself a facet of the private sovereignty of the individual and, thereby, a facet of the private sector and not the public sector.

The public sector, however, must not be denied its importance. Conservatives make a mistake when they deny the public sector any credibility, any authority, or any power whatsoever. We bash the government, we get angry with bureaucracy, and we let anger toward government boil to a fevered pitch. We sometimes stoke the opinion that any government is *too much* government. This is not the case! In fact, it would be *inconsistent* with logic itself to believe that the public sector should be ignored or denied respect.

In order to understand the public sector, however, one must understand society in general. By nature, there will be *no society whatsoever* that does not need rule by law. Within every aspect of society, there is a need for legality in order to ensure against *impediment,* for a set standard of good and bad that keeps the society as close to the *good* as possible. Hence, for this standard to matter, the people administer a governing body—or bodies—that they might oversee the rule by law and ensure a just society.

In order that it might properly protect the people, the government is also given the task of protecting their rights via the law. The founders pointed out this idea in the Declaration of Independence: "That to secure these rights governments are instituted among men." There is no better way to illustrate the role of the public sector than to candidly state the relation between itself and the people, via law and the rights of the people *protected by the law.* Law denotes the necessity of government—in other words—because government must uphold the law as a standard for society.

In order that both the private and the public sectors may stand in their respective positions, it becomes apparent that they must live in harmony with one another, while not overstepping their respective boundaries. In other words, the people must not try to obstruct justice, and the government must not try to obstruct the people's standing within the natural law. The private and public sectors are themselves what I consider harmonious opposites.

They are opposite in that the private sector is the *enactor* of natural rights, and the government is merely the guardian of these rights. Yet they are harmonious in that the public sector has been set in place in order to ensure the safety of the people in general, while the people are the ones being *protected.*

ELEVEN

Economic Principles, Stability, and Strength

Political Economy and Its Important Relationship to Limited Government

On Political Economy

Economics is often dismissed by average people as something they cannot fully understand. They believe that economics must be left to the trained economist, to the people running businesses, and to the government, and if all else fails, the economy must be left to the whims of the cosmos.

In fact, they are dead wrong.

There is an inherent and natural connection between economics and the individual. There is a direct correlation between the people, their economy, and their government—and thus the entirety of society. This idea is called *political economy.*

Jean-Baptiste Say defined it in his classic *A Treatise on Political Economy:* "The term *political economy* being now confined to the science which treats of wealth, and that of *politics,* to designate the relations existing between a government and its people and the relations of different states to each other."[1] Say is explaining that the government is not running the economy.

On the contrary, Say is merely trying to help the individual understand that the economy is run by neither the government nor the money crunchers, but that it is directed by every individual.

Say's point is the essence of this book's previous chapter on the private and public sector: Economically, socially, and physically, the private and public sectors must live in harmony. The government must be limited, and the people's rights must be protected from their enemies, foreign and domestic. If the public sector endeavors to become the *converse* instead of the *harmonious opposite* of the private sector, then problems will ensue. Specifically, if the government decides that it does not want to protect the private sector's sole right to create wealth, then the economy becomes drastically unbalanced and the economic structure favors government over the individual. Similarly, Say says that if the relationship is unbalanced and the government engages in action beyond its power, then the economy will be the worse for it. The balance of the economy is reliant on both the individual and the government existing in economic harmony. Say points out, moreover, that economics is a system that works within the *whole* balance of society, not the individual inner workings of one independent sector, but the interconnected workings of both sectors of society.

So the question is not whether government has a role in economics. Indeed, the conservative believes in a role for the public sector: to protect and preserve the individual's sole right to create wealth in the private sector. The real question for Say's statements on political economy is how *big* the government's role in the economy needs to be.

Moreover, just because the private sector is the wealth-creating sector does not mean that it is exempt from sound fiscal principle. On the contrary, because of its natural responsibilities in the creation and maintenance of wealth, the private sector must itself understand good fiscal principles just like the public sector.

The Production of Wealth

As mentioned in the previous chapter, the idea of wealth's creation is found in the private sector by both the laws of nature and the rights given to us by nature. A stable economy must be rooted in the individual because it is the individual that labors, and it is labor that creates Adam Smith's "real wealth."

This view on wealth means that individuals are responsible for gaining their own wealth and, therefore, have no reason to rely on the government for it. Wealth, the conservative believes, was never created in packs, herds, or mobs, but by the *person proper,* or, as we shall describe this person later on, the individual.

The person proper is the view of the human being closest to true natural law. In other words, it is the most natural, "proper" personification possible of each member of humanity. In considering the personification of this entity, we find the person proper to be not at all a loner, but merely someone who is himself or herself alone, not any other person, group of people, or nation. The rendering of this person proper is rooted in the person's independence, which makes the individual sovereign both in his or her own affairs and in the administration of all rights and freedoms due the person.

The person proper is not a member of some elite section of society, but an individual whose foremost goal is to fulfill his or her own American dream. That dream was never dictated to the person proper, but, like all dreams, started out as the person's own ideal and was achieved by personal hard work. The person proper does not stop here, but continues to work, toiling hard to preserve a dream and the natural rights and freedoms that enable all people to attain their dreams. The person proper, no matter the political ideology, thinks, speaks, and works for himself or herself. The person gives when he or she chooses, but wishes not to be excessively governmentally compelled (through taxation) to give money. The person proper is the independent individual. In economics, the person proper is understood to be the sole creator of wealth, because it is the individual as an independent human being who creates any economic prosperity. Because the individual is the true source of anything done in the private sector, the person proper must therefore be understood for who he or she is: the true source of both economic prosperity and wealth in any other format.

Wealth itself is not tangible, but the by-product of individual work and the trade of the land's fruit. Wealth pivots on two things: natural production and synthetic production.[2] Both kinds of wealth, in turn, are reliant on the person proper.

Natural products, or natural resources, can certainly survive on their own. But they create no wealth, staying stagnant in their natural format. The only way that these natural resources can create wealth is if the individual personally cultivates the land and tends to it and then makes a profit off its resources.

Oil, for example, falls under this category of natural products. The only way that such oil actually means anything as wealth is if the individual "cultivates" it. From this, we receive the necessity of the oil companies that first cultivate the land and then sell the natural resources into the market.

Thus, natural production is the private sector's act of cultivation of a nation's natural resources. Natural production is very important because, without the cultivation of natural resources, there is no synthetic production.

Without cutting down trees and selling them, the paper company wouldn't be able to manufacture. Without the "cultivation" of metal, the car companies couldn't build cars. As one can see, there is a heavy reliance of one on the other.

Synthetic producers are, as their name suggests, the producers of goods and services synthesized completely by human intervention. This is not to deny the idea that many synthetic products are based on natural resources—paper, for example—but these things are not cultivated per se by the synthetic producer but merely used by it. The synthetic producer buys such products from the *natural* producer. Therefore, synthetic production includes the majority of things that are marketed to the public, everything from pillows to stereo systems.

Of course, loan corporations, banks, stock exchanges, maids, gardeners, butlers, carpet cleaners, and things of this nature that are services within the economy are also aspects of synthetic law. These corporations and businesses are synthetic producers for the simple reason that they are the production of a service by human hands.

The Ideal of Capitalism

All of these principles are part of something that we can best refer to as economic theory. The conservative interpretation is best defined as the unchangeable law of the interchanging wealth between the people.

The principles of a given economic theory differ, depending on the economic system you adopt, but as long as you stay with a specific system, those theories are unchangeable. They do not shift with time, unless the entire system itself changes. For instance, the law of supply and demand doesn't change for a good or bad economic state! It is, being a sound business and economic principle, something that good businesspeople and economists will continue to use for the best interest of their own wealth creation.

There are, however, more versions of economic theory than one may think (or economic *systems,* as they are more consistently referred to). For example, the left believes in the Marxist theory of economics, a stated theory that because government must expand for the "good" of the changing society, so must the economy. In this manner, the neo/retro Marxist left embraces a philosophy that—as we have discussed—we might call state economic collectivism: the idea that the economic faculties of a given society are not truly *owned* by the individual but by the *state* and by the *government in general.* The conservative ideology embraces an economic ideology best described as capitalism.

Capitalism is best understood as resting on two pillars: wealth creation for the private sector and, second, a private sector free from dictation by the *public* sector. Capitalism is also distinctly defined by the idea of free trade.

Freedom from government. The three magic words have inspired people all over the world to stand up in opposition to oppression. Whether it be Poland's Solidarity movement, the

Sons of Liberty in America, or Great Britain's Oliver Cromwell and his Roundheads, throughout history, brave people have done brave things in order to preserve, gain, or continue their freedom from government.

TWELVE

Social Theory and Limited Government

Social Theory: Not Necessarily That Which Is Written, but Always That Which Is Known

Any proper examination of the theory of limited government must understand, as we have previously discussed, the natural relationship between the private and public sector. This relationship and—hopefully—this *harmony* denotes a relationship between the two sectors, which gives way to a certain bond that we call society; in fact, the harmonious relationship between the two sectors itself might very well be called society. This definition of society is based on the principle that the word *society* means the whole of humankind and not just one sector therein. This is not to say that society is the great equalizer, because the public sector will never have equivalent power to the private sector's natural rights. What this does say is simply that society is the great accord between the two. In other words, it is the harmony between the private and public sector that creates a good society—not the power of one over the other.

Society, however, is not without its own set of rules. To say that society denotes a mere crossroads between government and the people is absurd; indeed, it is nonfactual. While society as a

whole is in itself the harmony between the private and the public sectors and everything in between, such harmony is not without its own laws and ideals. To define these laws and ideals, we
must come up with a theory: a status quo, a statement of belief
that appeals to the whole of society's structure. This standard is
what we refer to as *social theory.*

To understand *conservative* social theory in particular, it is
best to think of it as an admixture of common sense, fact, the
written law, morality, and logic. Social theory is, in this manner,
not necessarily what is written, but always what is known and
deduced from the properties of reason and reality.

In other words, social theory covers things as obvious as the
sheer stupidity of crying "Fire!" in a crowded theater. This is
not necessarily written in the law, but it is known by the public
through common sense. Social theory can, however, cover
things as unobvious as the constitutional affirmation of the natural right of free expression as discussed in the First Amendment—this being covered in written law. Thus, social theory is
broad, and it covers both what a government bureaucracy is
needed for and what it is *not* needed for.

Social theory is volatile. It moves with society's improvements,
fads, and any other change in society itself so as to address these
new trends. It is only natural, then, that the government expansionist finds it an attractive arena in which to drive its agenda.
Marx himself wrote in his magnum opus *Das Kapital:*

> They do show that, within the ruling classes themselves, the
> foreboding is emerging that the present society is no solid crys-
> tal, but an organism capable of change, and constantly engaging
> in a process of change.[1]

In this much, Karl Marx has defined the social theory of the left: the idea that society, its actions, and any opinion on these things are based solely upon the mutations of the changing of ideas, ideals, thoughts, and actions of the society. One might easily state that this idea of change—based upon the theories of the changing dialectic that are all embraced by Marxists—leads to the conclusion of revolutionism: one of the basic pillars of the modern left.

All too often, people put their faith in change, hoping that societal shifts will improve their prospects. They believe that society's changes occur naturally and that social theory and the commonsensical thinking it all must be subverted to accommodate these changes. But to give way to this process of allegedly organic change is to forfeit everyone's security against Marxist reorganization of society.

Social Theory and the Victim Mentality

Five to four. That was the margin between the majority opinion and the dissent in the U.S. Supreme Court case of *Boy Scouts of America v. Dale (BSA v. Dale)*. The debate was between the private corporation that is the Boy Scouts of America and James Dale, a homosexual advocate for "gay rights." At issue was whether it was legal for the Boy Scouts to revoke Dale's adult membership and his position as an assistant scoutmaster.[2]

Dale complained that it was discriminatory for the BSA to revoke his adult membership. Thus the debate, on Dale's part, embraced the victim mentality: the mentality that—as discussed at the beginning of this book—implies a need for government to fix the indecencies and insults of an individual or group of individuals.

As described earlier, this mentality is Marxian both in concept and in practicality. After all, by coming to the government for something inconvenient and unaccommodating, you are giving government more sociological and, in the long run, physical power over you.

The victim mentality's use of the due-process clause as a means to embrace a left-wing social agenda is a misuse of it. The clause was created to protect the people from anyone wanting to harm them by allowing anyone to appeal to the judicial branch of government. The victim does not come for justice, however, but for vengeance against the unaccommodating, the inconvenient, and anyone who stands in his or her way. The "victimized" achieve this status not by means of true discrimination, but by either blowing out of proportion something trite until it seems like horrid discrimination or fabricating a horrible crisis in which the "victim" only seems to have suffered discrimination. The status of such a victim was evident in the case of *BSA v. Dale*.

The Boy Scouts of America's argument was simple "that homosexual conduct is inconsistent with the values it seeks to instill." BSA's position was simply that as a private corporation, it had a First Amendment right to maintain its organization's values and choose which individuals could promote those values through their freedom of speech and the succeeding right of "expressive association."[3] By accusing the BSA of discrimination—when they were simply embracing their right to association—Dale embraced the victim mentality.

After a long and arduous legal battle that began in New Jersey Superior Court and ended in the U.S. Supreme Court, the BSA's position was upheld.[4]

The American Civil Liberties Union (ACLU) espoused this view on the case the day of the decision:

> Anti-gay groups had hoped that a victory for the Boy Scouts would further fuel their efforts to secure broad exemptions from civil rights laws that bar discrimination in sexual orientation. The ACLU Lesbian and Gay Rights Project currently represents several cities and counties in such legal battles, ordinances or create broad exemptions in them.[5]

The ACLU gives a clever rejoinder to the conservative who was happy to see Dale lose to the letter of constitutional law under the First Amendment's right to free speech and succeeding "freedom of expressive association."

The ACLU's meticulous word modification defines those who opposed Dale as "anti-gay groups." This clever headshot aimed at the conservative is foul play. Conservatives are not anti-gay, but against the victim mentality.

The true debate was not about homosexuality, but about Dale's belief that his rights had been violated because a free and independent organization wanted to maintain its traditional values. The debate was about the BSA wanting to exercise its "freedom of expression" and a victim getting upset because he didn't get *his* way.

Individuals who embrace the victim mentality have a bad effect on society. The people who walk around our society believing they are perpetual victims of racism, sexism, or some other form of discrimination create a heavy burden on our legal system. Our court system is flooded with discrimination lawsuits when, in all actuality, someone has turned an "inconvenience" into an institutional "indecency."

The victim mentality creates its biggest burden on the society as a whole. There is a national consensus that discrimination is bad. But when used properly, discrimination can be itself a *good* thing. Obviously, assigning one or more groups of individuals to a status beneath the rest of society is harmful and wrong, and anyone defending such bigotry is rightly seen as a bigot, but is also labeled a discriminator. Bigotry and discrimination, however, can be two different things. An individual or group of individuals has the distinct right to *discriminate* in the sense that the individual or group of individuals chooses whom to associate and not associate with, so long as it does not cross the line from there to bigotry. The truth that the Boy Scouts have a right to discriminate in the way that they did, and yet are not bigots, is lost on much of the population.

Groups like the ACLU—who have an agenda behind all of this madness—delight in this confusion and seek to garner a favorable court decision from it.

All the while, those adhering to Marxian social theory are able to use the idea of *discrimination* and the victim mentality as tidal waves of change to position their agenda, and through the execution of this theory, the government expansionist inches closer to his or her goal of increasing the size of government along the lines of discrimination laws.

As previously mentioned, the victim is the government expansionist's ideal citizen, begging for government's help, unpleased with free expression by fellow individuals, and crying for change in society.

But what is the conservative to do when confronted by the victim mentality? The answer is simple, really. First, the victim is to be understood for who he or she is—a person whose worth is found in government. The conservative must actively promote the idea that each human being is an independent and sovereign individual. The social theory of individualistic independence is much stronger than the unproven *theory* of victimization; after all, independence is rooted in the rights and freedoms of society, while victimization is rooted in the power of an expansive government.

Second, the conservative must stand up against the victim mentality at every turn.

Furthermore, in analyzing social issues, in the case of the victim mentality, the moral law simplifies the solution for us: The victim mentality promotes the left's agenda, and the left's agenda denies—in retrospect—the moral code and natural rights. Therefore, the victim mentality is the denial of the moral code and natural rights.

Social Theory on That Which Is Typically Referred to as the Social Issue

The left's most effective attack on the conservative and his social theory is that conservatives want to "regulate you in your bedroom." Conservatives, according to the left, want to stop people from doing whatever they want in the privacy of their home. Often, we are accused of being antigay.[6] We are labeled antichoice on abortion, and antilife on the death penalty. The left feels that conservatives' most vulnerable spot is our often-misunderstood position on "social issues."

The conservative's perception of social issues is important to understand. First, you must understand that the conservative has no intention of making people the objects of social experimentation. In other words, the conservative is not interested in forcing the moral compass on anyone in the totalitarian or dictatorial sense in the manner that the left claims conservatives prefer.

On the issue of homosexual marriage, for example, conservatives are obviously opposed. They are opposed not because of the *legal* implications of marriage, but because of the moral implications of marriage. Morality, based upon reality, teaches us that marriage is deeply rooted in the nature of the family. As only the heterosexual marriage—marriage between a man and a woman—creates a traditional, possibly child-bearing natural family, the conservative follows up with the belief that homosexual "marriage" is not traditional and natural in the same sense. In other words, the conservative is not intolerant of the homosexual, but merely intolerant of adding to the moral law.

While the moral law is applied to the written law, it is *not to be a dictated standard*. The conservative has *no intention* of saying that homosexual partnerships should be illegal; the intention is simply to state that homosexual marriage—in the traditional formation of the word *marriage*—should be illegal. Conservatives believe that individuals are free to choose heterosexual or homosexual lives, as long as our cultural traditions on marriage are respected.

The so-called tolerant left claims that in order to have tolerance, one must first and foremost deny morality a stake or even a claim in the society. In doing such, any aspect of the moral law is itself deemed invalid or at least irrelevant. This brings to light a new morality with new standards created by government expansionism itself. The left can proudly claim that homosexual marriage is not in violation of the *new* morality.

Keep in mind, however, that the conservative is not in opposition *whatsoever* to the legal implications of homosexual relations. For one thing, the conservative is completely unopposed to civil unions, legal relationships between two individuals similar, but not identical, to marriage. The civil union is not a sacred moral bond, but merely a legal action and is therefore of no consequence to the moral compass.

It is clear that the "intolerance" of conservatism is not really intolerance. Because the definition of intolerance is completely relative to the definition of tolerance, and as the term is used by the left, tolerance is merely the agenda a certain political side has in mind; this makes "tolerance" entirely irrational! Moreover, by promoting morality over the synthetic law, the conservative is not "intolerant" but merely upholding *only* that which is in the best interest of society. Finally, to "tolerate" that which is not in the best interest of society hurts society; this becomes "intolerant" of the woes of the people.

For the preceding proofs we may conclude that Conservative social theory is morally bound: bound to set standards of good and evil that are unchangeable.

THIRTEEN

National Defense and Limited Government

Laws and Theories of Opposition, and the Foundation and Necessity of the Security of the State

Logic and common sense teach us that a key to staying physically alive is to not become "nonliving," or dead. Similarly, for the sovereign nation, the key to remaining economically, socially, and physically viable is staying alive. In order to protect the life of a nation in general—and its citizens in particular—a nation must be secure from its enemies who wish for the death of that nation and the body politic.

All independent entities have enemies. There will always be the hunter and the hunted. Such enmity between individuals and groups is not bad per se, but neither is such enmity good. It is, however, virtuous to disagree with opinions defying the moral compass. Naturally, the individual who believes in a moral foundation will have strong disagreements with whoever does not believe in morality. Similarly, whoever has an amoral foundation will have strong disagreements with whoever upholds morality.

All entities have enemies if for no other reason than there are opposing views on the moral law, and because the moral law is the basis of all law, there will be dissension everywhere.

Moreover, opposition can be either rational or irrational; often, it is the latter. Many people oppose something simply because they are told to oppose it. This is a kind of synthetic opposition, created by humans and not naturally part of the properties of philosophy. This is something I think is best referenced as the theory of *dictated opposition*, and it is often an important tool of the left. The theory of dictated opposition was never more evident than during the presidency of George W. Bush.

During the war on Islamic-fascist terrorism in the Middle East, Senate Majority Leader Harry Reid said on the floor of that august body, "This war is lost."[1] Time and time again after this, senator and representative alike repeated this mantra.

In defense of our lives, our soldiers gave the ultimate sacrifice. After September 11, 2001, when two planes plowed into two of the most prestigious and recognizable buildings in world economics, and when a third penetrated our national defense headquarters—on a day when our national sovereignty, independence, and safety were challenged by a foe whose aim was simply to humiliate, degrade, and destroy our morale, faith, and our principles—we Americans found ourselves united in love of country and love of natural rights. At such a time, when the balance is loss of freedom and possible loss of life versus loss of political arguments, the answer is simple and we revert to the natural tendencies of the former. But people don't think that way for long.

No, when Reid delivered the message that "this war is lost" in 2006—only three years before the United States would leave a new democratic government, which we helped establish, in the hands of the Iraqi citizenry—he and his colleagues had begun to figure out something devious. They had begun to realize that wartime emotions rise to a fever pitch and can easily be manipulated. Employing Marxian social theory, Reid and the left set out to push their agenda for change by using the antiwar movement as a convenient facilitator.

Therefore, when the left maintained that "this war is lost," their goal was not to communicate objective information to the people, but to instill a dictated opposition of the war in the minds of the people for its own political gain.

Dictated opposition has also often been used throughout history as a means of shifting the blame to someone who had nothing to do with the original problem. Whenever a king or queen was to blame for a problem, the ruler could either take the fall or dictate opposition as Reid did.

But true opposition is, as we have discussed, opposing because of disagreement. The war on Islamic-fascist terrorism was started, not because of disagreement but because of genuine hatred for us. Islamofascists hate America simply because as a nation, we believe in things that are in line with the moral compass. They are in direct contrast with the moral compass. Because they are in contrast with the moral compass, then, as adherents to the moral compass, we are in direct opposition to these terrorists.

War stems from dissension between two parties, and because there is always discord between the good and the bad, and between the politically driven and the freedom driven, we find that security for the moral freedom lover against any opposition becomes a necessity.

Therefore, we find the basis of security in the basis of war. All people have enemies, large or small. So all of us must have the capability to deal with these enemies on the appropriate scale. The conservative, who wants America to stay both a bastion of freedom and a bastion of morality, is thus compelled to secure the nation against enemies "foreign and domestic."

National Defense

The Constitution states: "The Congress shall have power to—provide for the common defense and general welfare of the United States—To raise and support armies—To provide and maintain a navy; To make rules for the government and regulation of the land and naval forces." We find that the national defense structure is a part of the public sector and an entity completely liable to the forces of the written law.

When one says that the government has power over the defense structure, one is giving the government enormous due. As with any aspect of government, there is always the potential for abuse, and as with many things, the government expansionist lives to erode boundaries.

This idea of government power over the defense of the nation does not, however, mean that there must be no boundaries for the government's defensive powers. Quite the contrary. In fact, the idea that government has power over a nation's defenses denotes that government must naturally *have* boundaries.

Because the private sector is the domain of the rights of the individual, and because the public sector has power over the national defense structure, the defense structure must itself not come into definite conflict with the rights of the individual. Recall the law of harmonious opposites as it pertains to the public and private sectors.

Moreover, because the two sectors must be different yet harmonious, it only follows that the national defense structure must not stay out of the way of the private sector's sole rights and powers, but it must also *preserve, protect, and promote* the free exercise of these rights and powers. In sum, part of the goal of national defense is to defend the rights and freedoms of the independent or sovereign human being.

National defense is not merely an aspect of the written law. It is the most important aspect of all law. If there is no defense, then the entire written law is worthless. If there is no defense, then economic law can very well be destroyed.

Defense, therefore, is the first priority of the conservative. After all, what use is law without its protection? Moreover, people say that money makes the world turn round, but what use is money if the nation is being destroyed? The answer in both cases is simply that the society, law, and money are all rendered useless.

As the nation is itself interchangeable with the philosophical idea of the national society, one can also argue that the defense of a nation is equivalent to the defense of the national society. Because the idea of a society is best defined as the private and public sector and their harmonious relationship, the protection of the national society must be the protection of the private and public sectors.

The idea of national defense has as its goal the protection of the rights of the individual, the preservation of the society as a whole, and the preservation of the separation between the private and public sector.

Conclusion

As one can see, there is a direct correlation between government and the national defense issue via the written law. From here, we can easily define ourselves according to certain lines of legal theory, but the same philosophical truth must remain, for the conservative: The government of a nation must live in harmony with the private sector.

Logically, to have effective national defense, one must actively support the strengthening of the national defense structure. If we are to have good national defense, the government must supply the military all that it needs to succeed without ceasing, because defense must be the number one priority of the society.

BOOK FIVE

Personal Responsibility and Individualism

FOURTEEN

Individualism

Individualism Versus Victimization

Society pivots on the individual. This is both a fact of life and a fact of nature.

As the individual is the only entity in society that can intelligently labor and, thereby, the only entity that can create wealth, the individual is the supreme power in the free market and the general economic system.

As the only entity in society that can engage in any thought process—no government, school, or any institution can think *for* you—the individual human being has supreme power over the formation of thought.

As each individual is the only entity in society that has any power whatsoever over his own actions—and the consequent decision of whether they are good or bad in relation to the moral compass—the individual is the deciding factor in any moral debate.

As the individual is the only entity in society that has the distinct ability to either obey or disobey the rule of law, an individual's actions become the focal point of interest in any legal decision.

As the sole recipient of natural rights, the individual is the key entity in any societal debate.

As the public sector's goal in the free society must always be to protect the interests of the citizenry of the society on the whole, and as the individual is the most basic aspect of the society's makeup, we find that the individual's *best interest* must be taken into consideration. For this reason, when any policy is proposed, the interests of the individual must always be thoroughly examined.

There can be no debate over whether the individual is the chief cornerstone on which society must be built. The person, and the person alone, holds the inherent rights of life, liberty, the pursuit of happiness, property, and the subsequent rights that stem from these basic ones (e.g., freedom of speech, the press, and religion, among others). An individual's independent association with these rights gives him or her an independent hand in their application.

Hence the facts of logic and philosophy prove that the individual alone is the chief entity within the society on the whole, in theory and in actuality. But these facts have not, however, been heeded by the left.

The most pernicious opponent to the individualistic mode of thought is the victim mentality.

There is strong and evident dissension between the victim and what the conservative realist sees as the evident individuality of the human condition. After all, if the victim were to embrace individuality, which states that the worth of the individual is found with the human being's own personal actions, then the idea of being a victim would become invalid. The person who embraces the victim mentality finds the worth he might find within freedom within government.

The condition of the individual is quite different from that of the victim. The victim is not his or her own person, but the government's person and, subsequently, the government expansionist's person. The individual *is* his or her own person, not conditioned, smoothed, or shifted by the whim of a government or political party. It is a difference of marked proportion: One screams for freedom *from* government; the other screams for interference *by* government.

One cannot hold a simultaneously positive view of the victim and the individual.

Moreover, the victim is reliant on the government. The government must, claims the victim, help with his or her inconvenience. The individual claims no such thing.

The victim is, to put it bluntly, a coward. Big Brother must be by his or her side for the victim to confront any problems.

The individual is a courageous person, believing in confronting problems on his or her own.

It is easy to see; the individual and the victim are polar opposites. They have opposite views of the person proper and opposite views of the human condition.

In the 1992 case of *Lee v. Weisman,* the U.S. Supreme Court ruled in favor of Daniel Weisman—the father of a Providence, Rhode Island, public school student—whose case was simply that prayer during a commencement ceremony (in which the attendees must stand) is a violation of the rights of the individual.

This case was part and parcel a culmination of years of many people's opposition to the idea of prayer—albeit even *nonsectarian* prayer—within public schools and other public-sector gatherings. Furthermore, this case was also partly the culmination of decades of left-wing utopian progressivism based upon the false premise that our nation is one of nontraditional values and non-Judeo-Christian ideals. Marx described religion and religious values as things to be fought against, describing this fight as "the struggle against religious illusions."[1]

This case was a turning point not just in social theory, but also in the interpretation of the Establishment Clause of the Constitution: "Congress shall make no law respecting the establishment of religion. ..." The opinion stated that having school prayer during a commencement ceremony is a violation of the Establishment Clause of the Constitution because it is—according to the Court—"religious exercise" on the premises of a government-funded organization.[2]

Justice David Souter wrote in his concurrence: "When public school officials, armed with the State's authority, convey an endorsement of religion to their students, they strike near the core of the Establishment Clause. However 'ceremonial' their messages may be, they are flatly unconstitutional."[3]

The flaw with Justice Souter's argument is self-evident: His point—which is also made by both his fellow concurrent Justice Blackmun and the opinion's author (Justice Kennedy)—is based upon the idea mentioned earlier that nonsectarian school prayer is a violation of the Establishment Clause. This is, however, a major logical fallacy, and—as Justice Scalia points out in the dissent—it is an argument with zero evidence to back it up.

The fact is, the Establishment Clause in its initial conception *does not* deny the right of a school to hold nonsectarian prayer during a commencement ceremony. It simply was meant (a) to stop taxes and other regulations from being used as a push for a religious agenda, such as had been experienced in Europe before the colonies fought for their independence, and (b) to stop the forced adherence to a certain school of theology. Scalia writes: "In holding that the Establishment Clause prohibits invocations and benedictions at public school graduation ceremonies, the Court—with nary a mention that it is doing so—lays waste a tradition that is as old as public school graduation ceremonies themselves, and that is a component of an even more longstanding American tradition of nonsectarian prayer to God at public celebrations generally."[4]

Justice Scalia makes a good point: You cannot make a true examination of an issue and deem it either constitutional or unconstitutional if you *do not look first to the original intent of the constitutional question at hand when the constitutional issue was written or ratified.*

Justice Scalia is, furthermore, correct in his conclusions. The emphasis of Judeo-Christian values on the society has a long and well-respected tradition.

From the tradition of marriage—recognized since the time of the colonies to be between a man and a women—to the tradition of prayer in public ceremony (when the Constitutional Convention got into its most spirited debates and the founders established a new practice of the chaplain within the body, an action that gave birth to a tradition of prayer at the beginning of Congress sessions), Judeo-Christian values have influenced society. Furthermore, in *County of Allegheny v. American Civil Liberties Union, Greater Pittsburgh Chapter,* Scalia and others acknowledged that "a test for implementing the protections of the Establishment Clause that, if applied with consistency, would invalidate longstanding traditions cannot be a proper reading of the Clause."[5] It is this point that Scalia makes pointedly and soundly.

Of course, Marxian social theory supports Souter, Kennedy, Blackmun, and the other loose constructionists in their decision. Marxian social theory's ideal that society's changes imply a change in our *standards for society* leads us to this observation: Seeing that society has changed since the Establishment Clause was written, so must our interpretation of it change in regard to school prayer. Moreover, Holmesian legal thought is in supreme agreement with this idea. We base our ideas—according to Holmes—upon *experience* and not upon *standards* or even *constitutional tradition:* We find this evident in *Lee v. Weisman.*

But the idea of *Lee v. Weisman* is, if nothing else, a great reward to the left's victims. One man who was insulted by two very short prayers at a commencement ceremony was able to bring down not only the Rhode Island School District, but also the entire nation's traditions and standards on prayer and set in place a more Marxian/Holmesian interpretation of prayer.

Individual Versus Universal

Aristotle wrote: "Some things are universal, others individual. By the term 'universal' I mean that which is of such a nature as to be predicated of many subjects, by 'individual' that which is not thus predicated."[6]

The idea of universality looms as a threat to the idea of individualism.

Proponents of institutionalizing society claim that it must become *part of* the government. Just as the victim believes in classifying inconvenience under the realm of government's protection of the individual against moral and ethical wrongs, the institutionalist wants to classify the individual under government.

Governmental expansion treats the person not as a separate, independent individual but as a mere speck within the populous and the society, not as a *member of* society—which denotes individuality *within* the whole—but as a *part of* society, which denotes a merging *with* the whole.

When integrated into a neo/retro Marxist society, the individual—like anything and anyone else—becomes a dependent of government, a subject of its dictation, and a slave to its every word. In this stage, the individual becomes an unwilling party to the institution and nothing else, merely a human being at the mercy of government instead of a separate individual. This creates a shift from the person proper in an individual sense to the person proper in a universal sense.

In creating an institutionalized society, one makes a rash decision that not only drastically changes the nature of the society, but also deals a serious blow to the person proper's status.

The conservative's opposition to institutionalization boils down to the most basic definition of the term *individual.* Moreover, the institution becomes merely a locomotive plowing the individual into the universal whole.

The purest and most basic format of individualism is the idea that the individual is himself or herself a distinct *member* of society. In turn, the institutionalization of society degrades the individual by turning a person into a piece of a universal whole.

Thus, we see that an object is either universal or individual, but never both. If a person is sovereign, separate, and independent in his or her own affairs—and thereby an *individual* human being—this individual cannot be a person in a universal sense at the same time. Both philosophy and logic forbid it! One must choose between a view of the human being as a sovereign member of the society or an individual merged in the universality of society.

The Foundations of the Individual

Individualism is a thought pattern in and of itself, and for this reason, it must have, as all viewpoints do, a philosophical foundation.

Individualism's foundation is based on a belief that individuals are the sole proprietors of *their* natural rights of life, liberty, the pursuit of happiness, and property, as well as subsequent rights such as freedom of speech, the press, and religion.

These rights, inherently given to the individual, are paramount to any understanding of individualism. The quality of the individual's standing in society rests on the sovereign power granted by these rights. Without them, the individual would be seen simply as a powerless member of society—powerless against government expansion and powerless against all authorities.

To deny the individual sole proprietorship over these rights is to deny the individual, in the long run, freedom from government expansion.

Moreover, the foundation of individualism falls under the category of his or her independence. This independence and sovereignty of the individual upholds the natural fact and self-evident truth that the individual is a separate entity of the national society from the government.

This argument is simple: The individual is an independent entity whose actions should be initiated by his or her own accord and not by the government.

Individualism and Personal Responsibility

There is one final precept of individualism. This is personal responsibility. The idea of personal responsibility is best defined as the individual's accountability for his or her actions—as opposed to leaving responsibility for these actions to someone else. It makes sense that individuals who are both independent and sovereign in their affairs must be, at the same time, independent and sovereign in the defense and punishment of their actions.

Moreover, responsibility is an aspect of the rule of law. In the justice system, the guilty party is summarily held responsible for a crime against the law. Only the guilty are responsible in the law, and the individualist believes that only the individual who engaged in an action should be held responsible.

This is not to say that the individual is only held responsible for wrongdoing. One is held responsible for everything that one does, good and bad.

Of course, the individual tries to shun responsibility's spotlight only on things that are considered bad. No one has a problem with taking responsibility for good actions.

Since the individual by human nature prefers to only take responsibility for what is perceived to be *good* and *moral* while trying to avoid responsibility for those things perceived to be *bad* and *immoral,* the individual who takes pride in morality will, most likely, be more *responsible* than someone who prides himself or herself on the denial of the moral compass. The realist or moral conservative will most likely take pride in individualistic personal responsibility more than the expansionist opponent will.

In understanding personal responsibility in relationship to individualism, we must understand that it is only the individual who can be held accountable and responsible. Only the individual can commit an action, and only the individual can be responsible for it. After all, a group of boys could be responsible for graffiti, but each of them *individually* is separately responsible for his personal engagement in the act.

The conservative individualist holds, for these reasons, that all individuals should be held accountable for what they have done—especially when it comes into conflict with the law.

The victim mentality shivers at this thought. The victim mentality cannot comprehend that an *individual* must be responsible for *the individual's* bad actions just as much as his or her *good* actions. It is a totally contradictory experience for the expansionist victim to acknowledge that *the victim* hurt someone with *his or her* actions; after all, is not this person supposed to be the victim, the hurt individual? Woe is you!

To claim responsibility for bad actions is an absurd thought for the individual embracing the victim mentality, because—to those who embrace this line of thought—everything is always somebody else's fault. What's more, the principle of the victim mentality implies that the *government* will take care of your grievances and, more specifically, your inconveniences. If *you* are held responsible for them, then what becomes of this idea?

The ultimate culmination of this is the simple question: Is personal responsibility a necessity for the individualistic conservative?

The answer is yes. It is an absolute necessity. If the individual is not responsible for his or her *own* actions, and someone else—such as the government—becomes responsible, then the individual's sovereignty is abridged. If the government becomes responsible for the individual's actions and inconveniences, then he or she gradually becomes reliant on the government's "help" and the government's ability to bail out individuals.

Personal responsibility is one of the most important precepts of individualism, because, without it, the entirety of individualism is unprotected.

FIFTEEN

Help Versus Protect

What Is the Government's Real Role?

To Help the Individual

On September 17, 2008, presidential candidate Barack Obama, speaking of his political agenda, claimed, "That's the change we need."[1]

His agenda proved to be nothing other than the change doctrine of Marxist law. Every policy he mentioned—from a universal health-care plan to cuts in national defense spending—was prefaced in his speeches by the promise that these changes would happen only if he were elected.

He spoke about a new society in which one could put one's "hope" in government. He spoke about how change in society was a necessity for progress, echoing Marx's idea that "the present society is no solid crystal, but an organism capable of change, and constantly engaging in a process of change." And he spoke about how the expansionist agenda was the right agenda for America.

On November 4, 2008, when the votes were counted, it seemed as though Americans had bought into Marxism and its change doctrine. It seemed that they wanted to use society to enact the left's political agenda. It seemed that the left had won the election, "hope," "change," and all. But the left had not won.

The people had in fact been tricked by Obama's intoxicating rhetorical flourish of change as a necessity. They heard promises about how government would benefit them—Obama's "Universal Preschool" plan, for example—and the people began to see this "change" in government as a glimmer of "hope" in what began to seem like a *dark,* very dark, world as Obama's rhetoric seeped into their minds.

By convincing the individual to hope in societal change, the Obama campaign was able to claim it had a mandate to change government, because the Marxist sees government as the only vehicle for changing society. Obama's policies, such as universal health care, perfectly reflected his own campaign statement that "when you spread the wealth around it's good for everybody."

The Obama campaign was able to turn the hope in its campaign promises into hope for a future Obama administration. Its campaign philosophy was, "Put your hope in *our* change; put your hope in government."

This change was promoted as "the change we need."[2] *If we need it, then it must be in our best interest to have it,* voters responded.

It becomes easy to transform systematically the minds of the people so they are receptive to the idea that more governmental power is in their best interest.

When confronted with the oppressive nature of this style of government, the expansionist panders to the people. The expansionist cannot portray "the change we need" as the Marxian change doctrine that it truly is. He or she must turn the unappealing expansionist ideology into a new appealing ideology.

One might call this new *appealing ideology* "the ideolo feelings."

The rhetoric that the expansionist uses to create this new form of the original viewpoint is absolutely empty. The pander is meaningless, and the words are completely and utterly worthless. This ideology of feelings is itself meaningless. It is a crafty appeal to bare emotions, an appeal to the heart of the electorate instead of its brain.

The ideology of feelings, also known as romanticism, maintains that the state's power is the ultimate goal of governance. Of course, this conflicts with the idea that the rights of the individual and their protection are the key to a good society, and therefore makes for a very *unappealing* view on government.

The expansionist must term it differently to attract support. Instead of government manifesting itself as the *ultimate* power in society, it must instead be cloaked as help for the individual.

For example, instead of admitting that universal health care is government's theft of the private sector's health-care industry, the romanticist brands it as free health care for the uninsured. Hence, the expansionist government appears to be a charity instead of a greedy power grabber in the eyes of the citizenry. Romanticism turns logic on its head, which is exactly what the government expansionist wants.

Barry Goldwater best encapsulated the expansionist's deception: "If you love your country, don't depend on handouts from Washington for your information. If you cherish your freedom, don't leave it up to BIG GOVERNMENT."[3]

Expansionists believe that people will begin to feel more and more comfortable with the gradual—or, in some cases, rapid—increase in the size and scope of government. The idea that you can simply *trust* government to do what is right corrupts the whole culture and society, turning the normal individual into a societal guinea pig created to endure the failed principles of governmental dependency.

The romanticist's claim that you can help the individual by expanding the size of government was shown to be bogus during the recent era of financial turmoil. In 1977, President Jimmy Carter reinstated a new version of an old law called the Community Reinvestment Act (CRA).[4] This law was certainly more than a reinvestment act; it was more a regulatory act forcing financial institutions to lend to at least a certain percentage of lower-income earners in their communities.

In part, the bill stated:

a. The Congress finds that—
   1. regulated financial institutions are required by law to demonstrate that their deposit facilities serve the convenience and needs of the communities in which they are chartered to do business;
   2. the convenience and needs of communities include the need for credit services as well as deposit services; and
   3. regulated financial institutions have continuing and affirmative obligation to help meet the credit needs of the local communities in which they are chartered.
b. It is the purpose of this title to require each appropriate Federal financial supervisory agency to use its authority when examining financial institutions, to encourage such institutions to help meet the credit needs of the local communities in which they are chartered consistent with the safe and sound operation of such institutions.[5]

In other words, bankers must meet the standards set by the government and demonstrate they are doing the government's bidding in their community, *or else.*

Over the years, several amendments to this act gave the government even *more* power over the people by creating an even more extensive body of regulating rules. Of course, the only reason the government enacted these extra rules was to create a more extensive regulatory system over lending institutions. And more regulation always means more *restriction* on an institution.

The CRA was originally concocted, in part, as an anti-discrimination measure to protect minorities seeking loans.[6] However, as the idea took shape, some government expansionists saw an opportunity to advance their agenda.

As written and amended, the CRA petrified many conscientious bankers who wanted to protect their investors' money. These men and women were afraid that the government would punish their institutions if they didn't lend to minority individuals who could not pay back their loans. Soon the floodgates opened, and scared bankers lent money to individuals of all races who could not afford to pay the institutions back. Then came 2008.

Banking institutions had been so badly wounded by the effects of government regulation from bills such as the CRA that they started to go into extreme debt. People couldn't pay back their loans, and banks couldn't get their money back. Soon these bad loans, or "toxic assets," began to poison the banking industry.

With an economic system hurt significantly by the CRA and other massive regulatory bills, the expansionists clearly failed in their stated mission—to help the people through the expansion of government.

No one was helped. Those who could not afford a home *still* couldn't afford a home, but many now owed a debt to the bank they could never pay back!

They might have been happy with their new home for a short while, but that happiness changed to dread when they found themselves in financial peril.

To Protect the Individual

When conservatives read, "secure the blessings of liberty to ourselves and our posterity" in the Constitution, they conclude that it means what it says. Furthermore, they conclude that while the *governed* are naturally supposed to adhere to the rule of law, set forth in the written format by a just government, the *government* is supposed to, in turn, protect the rights and freedoms that preserve the idea of individuality. It is as though the government shook hands with the people through the compact that is the Constitution. By ratifying what their representatives set forth in a purely republican format, the people created for themselves a valuable bargaining chip in the form of the Constitution. When the government tries to overstep its boundaries, the Constitution empowers the people to set it straight.

Hence the conservative finds it a natural belief that the government must not merely adhere to the Constitution, but also protect the Constitution so that the agreement between the private and public sector stays intact.

By protect, I mean securing and preserving something from another. So when the Constitution says that "[no individual shall] be deprived of life, liberty or property, without due process of law" the government is clearly mandated to protect the individual's natural rights from harm.

In this much, however, the government's job is simply to protect. The government's job is not to meddle and "fix" the individual, the national standard, and the individual's rights, but merely to *protect these things* in their original and most natural format.

The individual, in turn, must remain personally responsible. When a person acts within the boundaries of the law yet still makes the wrong decisions financially, socially, or in any other manner, it is the government's responsibility to refrain from taking action.

Once you as an individual allow government to meddle in the things that are your commission, you give the government more power than it is supposed to have and violate the constitutional agreement between the two.

And as the federal government's foray into American homeownership and lending practices has demonstrated, government expansionism leads not to happiness, but to the apparent need for more government expansionism.

EPILOGUE

America and Conservatism

If the United States were founded on the principles of institutionalization and government expansionism, instead of the natural rights of the individual—life, liberty, the pursuit of happiness, and property—then our nation would be markedly different.

Think about the institutionalist expansionist state. The government expansionist denies the natural law and the inherent rights of man in exchange for synthetic Marxian law.

If our nation had been based on government expansionism, the rights of every individual would be subjected to review by the institution, and only those aspects of the rights of man "beneficial" to the government would be acknowledged. Instead of living in a society in which the government is accountable to the individual, we would be living in a society in which the individual is accountable to the government.

There are some politicians and pundits who believe America would be better off under government expansionism. To them, I put this two-part question: Is America great, in their minds? And if it is, to invoke conservative author Dinesh D'Souza's defining question, "What's so great about America?"

Either America is great, or America is not great. If it is great, then wouldn't the reason for its excellence be its principles and foundational beliefs? No one ever says America is great because the government takes care of everyone. Immigrants are not drawn to this nation for the free social services, the way they are to Sweden.

If America is not great in someone's opinion, he or she likely believes we need a bigger and more expansionistic government in order to become better. The person probably wishes the United States were more like Sweden.

I believe that America is truly great. Indeed, I find it to be exceptional. It is the American Constitution and the *American* Constitution alone that has inspired nations abroad to design their governments to be subjugated to the rule of law and to the citizenry, equally.

It is the American enshrinement of freedom as a *right* that has made nations abroad draw themselves into the loving arms of republican government. It is the American experience within capitalism that has inspired other nations to adopt the economic principles on which our system was founded.

Freedom, capitalism, natural rights ... it is pure conservative principle on which our nation was founded, and when America succeeds, it is because of its original principles.

Acknowledgments

In the process of writing a work of this magnitude, it is inevitable that a number of individuals will come to light who deserve not merely a thank you, but also some public recognition.

I would first like to thank the incredible team at Vanguard Press for their dedication, devotion, and help. To Roger Cooper and Georgina Levitt, in particular, who helped me throughout the process: thank you for doing your job and doing it to the utmost extent.

I would also like to thank my wonderful mom, Marla, and dad, Doug, for putting up with me. Throughout the long days of writing and the long nights of editing, you were always there with love and support. I am more grateful than you could ever know.

I would like to thank my literary agent, Amy Hughes. Her continual advocacy for me throughout the *entire* process—and I mean *entire*—is something for which I owe her a deep debt of gratitude.

Furthermore, I owe endless thanks to my mentor and now colleague Dr. Bill Bennett. His support and encouragement since I got *involved* in politics has been important. His wise counsel as a friend is always welcome.

Thanks to Dr. Newt Gingrich, Rep. Tom Price, and Mike Gallagher for their support and advice throughout the process.

While I cannot thank *everyone* who has helped in some way or another, I can certainly say that the aforementioned persons are a sampling of the grand number of individuals I am blessed to have in my life. Daily I thank God for the opportunities He has given me and the people He has blessed me with. Thank you all so much.

Notes

Chapter One

1. Karl Marx and Friedrich Engels, *The Communist Manifesto* (New York: W. W. Norton and Company, 1988).

2. Ibid.

3. American Civil Liberties Union, "About Us," www.ACLU.org/About, accessed October 25, 2009.

4. Karl Marx, *Critique of the Gotha Program*.

Chapter Two

1. Plato, *Laws*, translated by Benjamin Jowett, http://classics.mit.edu/Plato/laws.1.i.html, accessed June 12, 2009.

2. Ibid.

3. Barack Obama campaign ad, "Out of Touch," www.youtube.com/watch?v=NZdi1JnMxFU&feature=channel, accessed June 12, 2009.

4. Alexander Miller, "Realism," in *The Stanford Encyclopedia of Philosophy*, fall 2008 ed., edited by Edward N. Zalta, http://plato.stanford.edu/fall2008/entries/realism/, accessed June 16, 2009.

5. Ibid.

6. C. S. Lewis, "Right and Wrong as a Clue to the Meaning of the Universe," in *Mere Christianity* (New York: Macmillan, 1943).

7. Ibid.

8. V. I. Lenin, *The Three Sources and Three Component Parts of Marxism* (Moscow: Foreign Languages Publishing House, 1959), 8.

Chapter Three

1. V. I. Lenin, *The Three Sources and Three Component Parts of Marxism* (Moscow: Foreign Languages Publishing House, 1959), 8.

2. Ibid.

3. Leslie Green, "Legal Positivism," in *The Stanford Encyclopedia of Philosophy,* fall 2008 ed., edited by Edward N. Zalta, http://plato.stanford.edu/archives/fall2008/entries/legalpositivism/, June 17, 2009.

4. M. and A. Black and Henry Campbell, *Black's Law Dictionary,* rev. 4th ed. (St. Paul, Minn.: West Publishing Company, 1957).

5. Ibid.

6. Aristotle, *The Nicomachean Ethics,* translated by David Ross and revised by J. L. Urmson and J. O. Urmson (Oxford: Oxford University Press, 1925; revised 1980), 24 and 115.

7. James Madison, *Notes of Debates in the Federal Convention of 1787 Reported by James Madison* (Athens: Ohio University Press, 1966), 197. (Note: This is just one instance in which the term "anarchy & tyranny" is employed.)

Chapter Four

1. Aristotle, *Rhetoric,* Great Books of the Western World series, edited by Mortimer J. Adler (Chicago: Encyclopedia Britannica, 1952; 1990).

2. California Secretary of State, Ballot Measure Information Page, 2000, www.sos.ca.gov/elections/sov/2000_primary/measures.pdf, accessed April 18, 2009.

3. Ibid.; California State Association of Counties, "The Creation of Our 58 Counties," www.counties.org/default.asp?id=77, accessed April 14, 2009.

4. California Secretary of State, Ballot Measure Information Page.

5. Judicial Council of California, "Supreme Court: High Profile

Case," www.courtinfo.ca.gov/courts/supreme/highprofile/, accessed April 14, 2009; and Judicial Council of California, "California Supreme Court Rules in Marriage Cases," press release, May 15, 2008, www.courtinfo.ca.gov/presscenter/newsreleases/NR26-08.PDF, accessed April 14, 2009.

6. In re MARRIAGE CASES, In the Supreme Court of California, filed May 15, 2008, available at www.courtinfo.ca.gov/opinions/archive/S147999.PDF, accessed April 14, 2009.

7. Ibid.

8. Ibid.

9. Oliver Wendell Holmes, *The Common Law* (Boston: Little, Brown, 1881, 1909).

10. Robert Scholes, "Strict and Loose Constructionism: A Decent Respect of the Opinions of Mankind," Brown University op-ed, October 13, 2004, www.brown.edu/Administration/News_Bureau/2004-05/04-037.html, accessed August 18, 2009.

Chapter Five

1. Office of the Governor of Texas, "Gov. Perry Backs Resolution Affirming Texas' Sovereignty Under 10th Amendment," press release, April 9, 2009, http://governor.state.tx.us/news/press-release/12227/, accessed August 17, 2009.

2. "Lone Star, Lone State?" *Countdown with Keith Olbermann,* www.msnbc.msn.com/id/26315908/#30235274, accessed August 18, 2009.

3. Ibid.

Chapter Six

1. Of course, this is incredibly stupid for a government to do. After all, the Soviets tried to govern without boundaries, and they ended up falling (and falling hard) in a war of international diplomacy as

well as economic, social, and national defense failure on their own home front.

2. Ronald Reagan, quoted in Gorton Carruth and Eugene Ehlrich, *The Giant Book of American Quotations* (New York: Gramercy, 2006).

3. Cornell University, Supreme Court Collection, *United States v. Butler,* www.law.cornell.edu/supct/search/display.html?terms= United%20States%20v.%20Butler&url=/supct/html/historics/USSC _CR_0297_0001_ZO.html, accessed August 18, 2009.

4. Ibid.

5. For "trade, traffic, or transportation," see Oregon Department of Transportation, State Motor Carrier Transportation Division, "What Is Interstate Commerce?" www.oregon.gov/ODOT/MCT/ docs/InterstateCommerce.pdf, accessed August 18, 2009.

6. Cornell University, Supreme Court Collection, *United States v. Butler,* www.law.cornell.edu/supct/search/display.html?terms= United%20States%20v.%20Butler&url=/supct/html/historics/USSC _CR_0297_0001_ZO.html, accessed August 18, 2009.

7. Ibid.

8. Ibid.

Chapter Seven

1. Percy Bysshe Shelley, *The Triumph of Life,* in University of Toronto, Representative Poetry Online, http://rpo.library.utoronto. ca/poem/1912.html, accessed August 17, 2009.

2. Aristotle, *Nicomachean Ethics,* Book I, translated by Benjamin Jowett, Massachusetts Institute of Technology Online, http://classics. mit.edu/Aristotle/nicomachaen.1.i.html.

Chapter Eight

1. Evan Thomas, "The Case for Killing Granny," *Newsweek,* Sep-

tember 12, 2009, www.newsweek.com/id/215291/page/1, accessed October 19, 2009.

2. Quote from ibid.

Chapter Nine

1. Mark Hill, "Carnegie Stages," University of New South Wales, Department of Medicine, http://embryology.med.unsw.edu.au/wwwhuman/Stages/Stages.htm, accessed July 12, 2009.

2. Karl Marx and Friedrich Engels, *The Communist Manifesto* (New York: W. W. Norton and Company, 1988).

3. Ibid.

4. *Roe v. Wade,* January 22, 1973, www.tourolaw.edu/Patch/Roe/, accessed July 12, 2009.

Chapter Ten

1. Adam Smith, *The Wealth of Nations,* modern library ed. (New York: Random House, 1994).

2. Cornell University, Supreme Court Collection, *Kelo v. New London,* www.law.cornell.edu/supct/html/04-108.ZO.html, accessed August 27, 2009.

Chapter Eleven

1. Jean-Baptiste Say, *A Treatise on Political Economy; or the Production, Distribution, and Consumption of Wealth,* translated from 4th ed. by C. R. Prinsep (Philadelphia: Lippincott, Grambo, 1852), available at University of Michigan University Library Web site, http://quod.lib.umich.edu/cgi/t/text/text-idx?c=moa;idno=AJB6576.

2. This idea is best reflected in Smith, *Wealth of Nations;* for example, "the annual produce of the land and labour of the society."

Chapter Twelve

1. Karl Marx, *Das Kapital,* 4th ed. (1890), available at www.econ. utah.edu/~ehrbar/cap1.pdf, accessed July 23, 2009.

2. The discussion in this section is based on information from www.law.cornell.edu/supct/html/historics/USSC_CR_0530_0640_ZS.html, accessed July 23, 2009.

3. Cornell University, Supreme Court Collection, *Boy Scouts of America v. Dale,* June 28, 2000, www.law.cornell.edu/supct/html/historics/USSC_CR_0530_0640_ZO.html, accessed July 23, 2009.

4. Ibid.

5. American Civil Liberties Union, "U.S. Supreme Court Ruling That Boy Scouts Can Discriminate Is 'Damaging but Limited,' ACLU Says," June 28, 200, www.aclu.org/scotus/1999/11988prs 20000628.html, accessed August 27, 2009.

6. Ibid.

Chapter Thirteen

1. Fox News, "Reid: Someone Tell Bush the War in Iraq Is Lost," April 19, 2007, www.foxnews.com/story/0,2933,267181,00.html, accessed August 27, 2009.

Chapter Fourteen

1. Karl Marx and Friedrich Engles, *The German Ideology, Including Theses on Feuerbach* (Amerherst, NY: Prometheus Books, 1998).

2. Cornell University, Supreme Court Collection, *Lee v. Weisman,* www.law.cornell.edu/supct/html/historics/USSC_CR_0505_0577_ZO.html, accessed October 31, 2009.

3. Ibid.

4. Ibid.

5. Cornell University, Supreme Court Collection, *County of Al-*

legheny v. American Civil Liberties Union, Greater Pittsburgh Chapter, www.law.cornell.edu/supct/html/historics/USSC_CR_0492_0573_ZS.html, accessed November 3, 2009.

6. Aristotle, *On Interpretation,* http://classics.mit.edu/Aristotle/interpretation.1.1.html, accessed August 21, 2009.

Chapter Fifteen

1. Barack Obama, "The Change We Need," remarks made in Elko, Nevada, September 17, 2008, on the Organizing for America Web site, www.barackobama.com/speeches/index.php, accessed August 27, 2009.

2. Ibid.

3. Barry Goldwater, quoted in Gorton Carruth and Eugene Ehlrich, *The Giant Book of American Quotations* (New York: Gramercy, 2006).

4. U.S. Congress, Community Reinvestment Act of 1977, www.fdic.gov/regulations/laws/rules/6500-2515.html.

5. Ibid.

6. Eric Rosengren and Janet Yellen, foreword to *Revisiting the CRA: Perspectives on the Future of the Community Reinvestment Act,* Joint Publication of the Federal Reserve Banks of Boston and San Francisco, February 2009, www.frbsf.org/publications/community/cra/.

Index